Research in Learning
and Teaching
in Educational Leadership

A Volume in
UCEA Leadership

Series Editors:
Michelle D. Young, *University of Virginia*
Liz Hollingworth, *University of Iowa*

UCEA Leadership

Michelle D. Young and Liz Hollingworth, Series Editors

*At a Crossroads: The Educational Leadership
Professoriate in the 21st Century* (2011)
by Donald G. Hackmann and Martha M. McCarthy

*Snapshots of School Leadership in the 21st Century: Perils and Promises
of Leading for Social Justice, School Improvement, and Democratic Community
(The UCEA Voices From the Field Project)* (2012)
Edited by Michele A. Acker-Hocevar, Julia Ballenger,
A. William Place, and Gary Ivory

Research in Learning and Teaching in Educational Leadership (2014)
edited by Liz Hollingworth and Arnold Danzig

Research in Learning and Teaching in Educational Leadership

Edited by

Liz Hollingworth
University of Iowa

and

Arnold Danzig
San Jose State University

Information Age Publishing, Inc.
Charlotte, North Carolina • www.infoagepub.com

Library of Congress Cataloging-in-Publication Data

CIP data for this book can be found on the Library of Congress website
http://www.loc.gov/index.html

Paperback: 978-1-62396-508-2
Hardcover: 978-1-62396-509-9
E-Book: 978-1-62396-510-5

Printed in the United States of America

CONTENTS

ABOUT THE LTEL SIG KOTTKAMP AWARD

Each year, the Learning and Teaching in Educational Leadership (LTEL) Special Interest Group (SIG) recognizes a recent doctoral graduate (PhD, EdD) whose research, evaluation, or scholarship aligns with the LTEL SIG goals, mission, and purpose through the Robert Kottkamp Outstanding Dissertation Award. Only dissertations completed during designated year that investigate educational leadership preparation and development programs, assess the impact of preparation on leadership practice, examine policy issues related to state or national leadership standards assessment and credentialing, or contribute through disciplined inquiry to the knowledge base about learning and teaching in educational leadership will be considered. Studies embracing both traditional and alternative conceptualizations and methodologies are welcomed.

LTEL SIG brings together professors and graduate students of educational leadership and administration, discipline specialists, educational theorists, curriculum developers, instructional technology specialists, learning specialists, educational researchers, classroom experts, practitioners, policymakers, and others concerned with learning and teaching in educational leadership. The LTEL SIG provides a forum for:

- a managed conversation on issues related to learning and teaching in educational leadership and administration;
- the integration of theoretical quantitative and qualitative studies of learning and teaching in educational leadership;
- discussion of investigations conducted in real educational settings, including investigations involving application of technology to learning and instruction;

Research in Learning and Teaching in Educational Leadership
pp. vii–viii
Copyright © 2014 by Information Age Publishing

- exploration of innovative methodologies;
- analysis of the implications of research and practice for learning and teaching in educational leadership; and
- assessment of the relationship of learning and teaching.

CHAPTER 1

INTRODUCTION

Learning and Teaching
in Educational Leadership

Arnold Danzig

ABSTRACT

This introductory chapter in *Research in Learning and Teaching in Educational Leadership* provides an explanatory framework for educational leadership and contextualizes the research which follows. The chapter briefly summarizes some of the discussions that have been part of conversations about educational leadership among members of the Learning and Teaching in Educational Leadership (LTEL) Special Interest Group, which is a sponsored subgroup of the American Educational Research Association. The discussion which follows explores how the name of the sponsoring Special Interest Group has changed, and how these changes reflect orientations in the field of educational leadership. The chapter concludes with brief mention of some of the core commitments of the doctorate in education and provides context for understanding how the research reported in subsequent chapters fulfill the goals of doctoral programs in educational leadership.

Research in Learning and Teaching in Educational Leadership
pp. 1–14

WHAT'S IN A NAME? TEACHING IN EDUCATIONAL ADMINISTRATION (TEA) TO THE LEARNING AND TEACHING IN EDUCATIONAL LEADERSHIP (LTEL) SPECIAL INTEREST GROUP

In 2008, the name of the Special Interest Group that sponsors the Kottkamp Doctoral Dissertation Awards achieved by the chapter authors was changed from *Teaching in Educational Administration* (TEA) to *Learning and Teaching in Educational Leadership* (LTEL). While some SIG members may remember the name change, it is worth briefly discussing the arguments that were used to justify the name change and how the name serves as context for the research presented in this volume.

Administration to Leadership

While the change from administration to leadership may not appear to be a significant change, it does reflect years of discussion about the meaning of school administration, and evolution of roles of the people who serve in formal and informal leadership positions in schools. The popular usage of the terms administration and management are also relevant to this discussion.

Most business schools (or schools of management), offer the MBA or master's of business administration as its terminal degree, while the training for managers in the public sector culminates in the MPA or master's of public administration. Both degrees are awarded to practitioners, and recognize the largely applied nature of their work, in leading and managing organizations and agencies, public, private, and nonprofit. Likewise, the master's in educational administration was the prototypical degree awarded to those moving out of teaching into the ranks of administration as assistant principals, principals, business managers, human resource directors et cetera. Some critics of school administration preparation programs (Hess & Kelly, 2005; Levine, 2005) have argued that there is a disconnect between what is taught in graduate programs in educational administration and the real world skills needed to lead a school or school district.

In one sense, the use of term "administration" prioritizes practical skills and functions of managers related to how organizations actually operate (see for example Chester Bernard's [1938/1968] classic, *The Functions of the Executive*). At the highest levels, the school administrators were considered to be executives (chief exectuive officers), more aligned with their colleagues in the business community, than those thought to have a calling and serving the public good.

Bennis (2003) distinguished between leadership and management: the latter was more concerned with the day-to-day "running" of the organization, while leadership was more associated with charting the direction for the school or organization. The metaphor of "ships captain" illustrates this distinction, with the person charting destination more of the leader and the person steering the boat considered to be the manager. While the distinction has been overblown, and there is now more recognition that effective people do both nuts and bolts details as well as chart the course, the distinction nevertheless holds in popular literature on leadership. Administration is usually more closely aligned with the management perspectives.

A second thread in explaining the move away from the term administration toward the term leadership is explicit in the writings on the moral commitments of those who lead schools (Heifetz, 1994; Sergiovanni, 2001; Starrett, 2007; Terry, 1993), who explicitly reject the priority on business functions and instead see a moral basis for practice, arguing that school administrators should be moral leaders, setting guiding purposes, establishing vision and mission, in order to establish themselves as leaders.

Senge (1990) argues that stewardship is particularly related to educational leadership. He draws on the ideas taken from Greenleaf (1977/1991) and argues that a leader is a servant first, and that the commitment to serve is part of the choice that leads one to aspire to lead; this commitment is different than someone who is driven to lead because of the desire for power or desire for material possessions. Senge's notion of the education leader as steward works on two distinct levels: (1) stewardship for the people being led, and (2) stewardship for the larger purpose or mission that underlies the enterprise of education.

Leadership Effects: Interdependence and Indirect Influences

The switch from administration to leadership also implies a deeper understanding of how educational leadership is connected to learning. According to an Organisation for Economic Cooperation and Development Report (Pont, Nusche, & Moorman, 2008), "the overall conclusion emerging from the more than 40 studies … is that school leaders have a *measurable, mostly indirect influence* (italics in original) on learning outcomes. This means that the impact of school leaders on student learning is generally mediated by other people, events and organizational factors such as teachers, classroom practices and school climate" (Hallinger & Heck, 1998, as cited in Pont et al., 2008, p. 33). The report goes on to argue that these elements contribute interdependently to the enactment of leadership tasks. Their conclusion is that the power of the school leader is "helping to create the conditions for effective teaching and learning. School leaders influence the motivations, capacities and working conditions of teachers who in turn shape classroom practice and student learning" (pp. 33-34). Pont et al. (2008) highlight the view that leadership is not only found in the office of the school principal, but is distributed throughout the school organization. "*Leadership* is a broader concept where authority to lead does not reside only in one person, but can be distributed among different people within and beyond the school. School leadership encompasses people occupying various roles and functions such as principals, deputy and assistant principals, leadership teams, school governing boards and school-level staff involved in leadership tasks (Pont et al., 2008, p. 18).

In a second volume of the Organisation for Economic Cooperation and Development report, Elmore (2008) suggests that leadership in schools flows from expertise about learners and learning and less on formal or positional authority. While Elmore prioritizes the improvement of instructional practice, his school leaders view learning as a collective good in which leaders model and exemplify the values and behaviors they want others to adopt. According to Elmore (2008)

- Instructional improvement requires continuous learning by all and distributed leadership needs to create an environment that views learning as a collective good.
- Leaders lead by exemplifying the values and behavior they want others to adopt.
- The roles and activities of leadership flow from the expertise required for learning and improvement, not from the formal dictates of the institution.
- The exercise of authority requires reciprocity of accountability and capacity. Overall, leadership roles based on expertise and reciprocity of accountability are those that best create the conditions for organizational learning that is the sine qua non of large scale reform in schooling (Elmore, 2008, cited in Pont et al., 2008, p. 83).

Elmore's (2008) principles resonate well with the switch from administration to leadership: (1) leaders develop practices which value and engage learners, (2) learning is everyone's responsibility, not something that is expected only from children or students, and (3) leaders inquire into their own learning; they explore how to use information to acquire new skills and accomplish tasks that they deem are important in their work and in their lives.

Focus on Learners as a Requirement of Educational Leadership

Almost 100 years ago, Dewey (1916) criticized the view that school is a preparation for life and instead pointed to a more immediate connection between the learner and engagement in meaningful activities at school. Freire (1970) also criticized school curricula and assessment practices which embrace a "banking concept" of education, where knowledge and learning were more like a deposit for future use than an opportunity to think about, even solve problems. Likewise, a "funds of knowledge" approach (Gonzalez, Moll, & Amanti, 2005) points to the importance of relevant curriculum and how the knowledge and skills that children (and families) bring to school are the starting places for learners and for building a richer school curriculum.

Consideration for learners and the ways people learn adds to the role and responsibilities of school leaders; it also implies greater concern for the social, cultural, historical experiences that learners bring to their educational experiences. The American Psychological Association (1997) articulated *Learner-Centered Psychological Principles: A Framework for School Redesign and Reform,* as part of an initiative that explored how people learn and which outlined multiple principles of learner-centered environments. The use of the term *learner-centered* was also part of a report by the National Research Council (2000): *How People Learn: Brain, Mind, Experience, and School.* The report identified four different learning environments (*learner-centered, knowledge-centered, assessment-centered,* and *community-centered*), each with its own assumptions and emphases. The learner-centered approach prioritized the need for learners to control their own learning as they define learning goals and monitor progress in achieving them. Freedom, self-direction, and relevance were described as primary factors affecting motivation and the ways in which people learn.

Applications to Learner-Centered Approaches to Leadership. One of the earliest applications of learner-centered principles to school leadership came in a chapter titled "A Culture in the Making: Leadership in Learner-Centered Schools" by Lieberman, Falk, and Alexander (1995), which appeared in the 94th National Society for the Study of Education Yearbook, *Creating New Educational Communities: Schools and Classrooms Where all Children Can Be Smart* (1995). According to Lieberman et al. (1995, 2007), the concept of learner-centered leadership is built on the foundation where "the purpose of education was to create the conditions for student development and autonomy while establishing a pattern of support for continuous progress within a school community nurtured by a democratic ethic" (Lieberman et al., 2007, p. 26). Lieberman et al. (1995, 2007) point out there are multiple roles required of school leaders which embrace a learner-centered approach: educators, problem solvers, crisis managers, change agents, enablers, consensus builders, and networkers. The learner-centered leader gives meaning to the many ways that the day-to-day activities of participants contribute to school and organizational purposes, with the aim of connecting individuals to the wider community of learners. Learner-centered leaders translate guiding ideas into educational practices that engage all members of the community. Robinson (2011) uses the term student-centered leadership to contrast management approaches from the decisions and actions that school leaders take to promote student learning. She asks "do the decisions and actions of the school's leadership improve teaching in ways that are reflected in better student learning, or is their focus so far removed from the classroom that leadership adds little value to student learning" (p. 4)?

Learner-centered leadership (Danzig et al., 2007; Danzig, 2009) extends the idea of being a learner from its focus on children and students, to the adult participants in educational settings: staff, teachers, administrators, parents, and community members. This approach assumes that leadership is not only found in the principal's office and that many others bring knowledge, experiences, and leadership to the wide variety of duties and responsibilities that are associated with schooling. The description and use of the term *learner-centered* leadership suggests that the work of leading involves being a learner. Being a learner also implies voluntary and reciprocal relationships and a reduction in hierarchy and formal status. Learner-centered leaders give priority to democratic structures and relationships, and see the need to negotiate the terms of success for individual efforts as well as for institutional norms. The learner-centered school principal is less of a production manager and more engaged in acts which lead to new understandings of self, others, context, and environment, creating spaces for others to do the same. Learner-centered leaders recognize the importance of social relations in schools, and how social relations affect not only individual learners, but also contribute to systems operations.

A conceptual framework for school leadership that places value on learners and on learning raises important questions about schooling and the expectations for school leaders: Chapman (2008) asks:

- What are accepted as significant outcomes of schooling?
- What learning outcomes can schools reasonably be expected to achieve, given factors such as student background, socioeconomic status and family commitment to education?
- What school outcomes can be reasonably expected given different levels of resources, school mission focus and type of school (public or private)?
- What learning is most valued?

- Whose learning is valued—that of students, teachers, the school community?

Often cited calls for high expectations should not be viewed uncritically, as something that is good for all learners, at all times. Expectations that are too high can be unrealistic and defeating. Schools are critical places already, and a culture of high expectations can change into a place where overly critical adults focus on what children cannot do instead of what they can do. Working to fulfill the "high expectations" of others leads to an emphasis on external rewards as opposed to intrinsic satisfactions; short term achievement gains may sacrifice long-term possibilities, and feelings of resentment (for those who do not meet expectations) or entitlement (for those who do) The corollary, criticizing schools for low expectations, especially schools with large numbers of students living in stressed economic conditions, misses the ways that poverty creates problems for children and adults in schools. Often, the problems in schools serving poor children are not necessarily based in lower expectations, but the result of fewer resources, greater needs and costs, and mismatch between the expectations at school and the opportunities that are available in life. Rather than focusing on high expectations, a better strategy is to look at the factors that limit life chances and doing something to mitigate their effects. The risk is that the demand for "high performance expectations" in schools will lead learners to internalize their failure and blame themselves for how the system failed them. Dropout rates in urban schools of 30%-40% and higher, confirm these risks. Too often, the corporate model of education explains learning as something to be efficiently and productively managed and assessed. High standards, rigorous curriculum, quality instruction, performance accountability (four of the core components of school performance) adopt business language which treats learners as objects to be controlled, manipulated, and filled, instead of as participants in their own education and learning.

Real world contexts are also prioritized in this view of leadership. Seeing leaders as learners opens up the space for school leaders to build their own curricula, and to question what needs to be learned in order for them to accomplish individual goals and organizational responsibilities. Individual hopes and organizational tensions are connected, which provide the impetus to learning, and learning from experience. When learners are valued, schools create opportunities for personal experience to be explored, extended, and applied. The valuing of personal experience requires that tacit knowledge become manifest and that learners have opportunities to explore their own stories and experiences. Personal knowledge is forged in the experiences that people have and in their interactions with others (Polanyi, 1962, 1967). Drawing from personal knowledge requires reflection, as a means of processing information and connecting personal understandings to new knowledge (Danzig, Blankson, & Kiltz, 2007; Danzig, Borman, Jones & Wright, 2007; Putnam, 1991; Schön, 1991; Sergiovanni, 2001). Learners are enhanced when they have opportunities to interact and to collaborate with others on meaningful tasks. This view of leadership suggests the need to create respectful settings in which diversity and diversity of thought are encouraged through social interaction and meaningful dialogue. People learn as they participate with a community of learners, interacting with that community and understanding and participating in its history, assumptions, and cultural values and norms. Learning in school requires that learners are valued at school. Placing value on personal and tacit knowledge gives new meaning to assessment, evaluation, and accountability efforts in schools and the roles played by education leaders.

The work of education leaders is to move beyond technical approaches for maximizing human learning (and quantifying human experience) and instead looks at how people achieve value in their lives and in how they learn from experience. The use of readability scales, for example, which represent a book by a lexile score and then match books for children at their 'appropriate reading level" fundamentally misses the way the children decide to read and enjoy books in their lives. If I had followed this technical approach, I might never had read the Harry Potter books to my daughter, who in turn may never have used the Potter books to motivate herself to learn to read, much less enjoy reading the whole series of books, watch the movies, collect artifacts, and engage in hundreds of conversations with peers and adults. Technical approaches often fail to reveal how the measurement metrics are often quite imprecise, and do little to explore what it is that one must do in school or life, based on what the metric says. The measuring act itself damages those who inevitably come up on the lower end of the scale. Focusing on student attendance, for example, inevitably leads to penalizing children for not being in school; it justifies the penalties both formally and more implicitly, through internalizing a norm that it is unfair to treat children who show up every day the same way as those who don't come as regularly, regardless of what is experienced and learned outside of school. The ratings used to compare children, teachers, administrators, schools, districts, are very different from the popular interpretations and meanings given to these ratings.

Research on Educational Leadership: Person, Contexts, or Both

One final question concerns whether the qualities of leaders which should be the focus of our future research studies, or whether it is the situation or context which primarily determines the quality of leadership needed for successful schools. An exchange of letters about the study of leadership between Robert Sternberg and Victor Vroom (2002) provides the opportunity to consider the question concerning whether leadership research should focus on the person, the situation, or both. Sternberg's research on leadership starts by looking at the traits and skills of those leaders, focusing more on the leader as a person. His model is based on what he calls WICS: wisdom, intelligence, and creativity **synthesized** (emphasis in original) (Sternberg & Vroom, 2002). Sternberg does not necessarily believe that people are born with these qualities or attributes; rather, they are the result of interactions with the environment that draw from or utilize innate potentials. Some people are better able to do this, while others are less successful. Sternberg also recognizes that leadership responsibilities are usually ill-defined and dynamic without any fixed algorithms or solution sets to which a leader can routinely follow. This is similar to the point made by Heifetz (1994), in which he distinguishes problems which require "adapative" as opposed to "'technical" solutions. Outcomes are often unclear, and goals and methods usually emerge over time. Sternberg also emphasizes practical intelligence. "Practical intelligence is the ability to solve everyday problems by utilizing knowledge gained from experience in order to purposefully adapt to, shape, and select environments. It thus involves changing oneself to suit the environment (adaptation), changing the environment to suit oneself (shaping), or finding a new environment within which to work (selection). One uses these skills to (a) manage oneself, (b) manage others, and (c) manage tasks" (Sternberg & Vroom, 2002, p. 303).

The second criterion for leadership identified by Sternberg is creativity.

Creativity refers to skill in generating ideas and products that are (a) relatively novel, (b) high in quality, and (c) appropriate to the task at hand. Creativity is important for leadership because it is the component whereby one generates the ideas that others will follow. A leader who is practically intelligent may get along and get others to go along—but he or she may get others to go along with inferior or stale ideas. Many leaders are academically and even practically intelligent, but uncreative, essentially leading people through their ability to influence rather than through their agenda. (Sternberg & Vroom, 2002, p. 303)

According to Sternberg,

The various forms of creative contributions engender different kinds of leadership. In particular, some leaders transform the nature of an organization or other institution, whereas others do not. At a given time, in a given place, transformation may or may not be called for. So transformation is not necessarily needed in every leadership situation. But the leaders who tend to be remembered over the course of history are probably, in most cases, those who transform organizations or, more generally, ways of thinking. (Sternberg & Vroom, 2002, p. 305)

The third leadership criterion that Sternberg recognizes is wisdom. Sternberg suggests that

an individual is wise to the extent he or she uses successful intelligence as moderated by values to (a) seek to reach a common good, (b) by balancing intrapersonal (one's own), interpersonal (others'), and extrapersonal (organizational/institutional/spiritual) interests, (c) over the short and long term, to (d) adapt to, shape, and select environments.... Rather, they skillfully balance interests of varying kinds, including their own, those of their followers, and those of the organization for which they are responsible. They also recognize that they need to align the interests of their group or organization with those of others groups or organizations because no group operates within a vacuum. Wise leaders realize that what may appear to be a prudent course of action over the short term does not necessarily appear so over the long term. (Sternberg & Vroom, 2002, p. 305)

Vroom responds by suggesting that it is the situation rather than the person which deserves greatest consideration in understanding leadership. "I stand by a statement that I made over a quarter of a century ago that it makes more sense to talk about autocratic situations than autocratic managers" (Sternberg & Vroom, 2002, p. 316). Vroom concludes that it is both the leadership qualities of the individual and the situation which ultimately matters. Vroom adds that "Perhaps we both can agree that matching of personal qualities and situational requirements is critical to leader effectiveness. However, each of us focuses on a different part of that match (Sternberg & Vroom, 2002, p. 311).

Sternberg responds that

I think we agree that the person, the situation, and the interaction of the person with the situation (and the task confronted in the situation) all matter for leadership effectiveness ... I think we must both try to understand leaders in interaction with their environments, or sooner or later, both our theories will fail. In the long run, of course, all theories of leadership (or anything else) are replaced by better theories. The most important question therefore is how generative one's theory will be in leading to the theory or theories that ultimately replace(s) it! ... Again, it is the interaction of the individual with the situation, and not just the individual or the situation, which determines leadership effectiveness. (Sternberg & Vroom, 2002, p. 314)

Sternberg concludes that

We view both individuals and situations as important and interfused; we view knowledge, including tacit knowledge, as neither wholly domain specific nor wholly domain general, but as varying on a continuum between the two; and we view instruction and assessment as equally important and also interfused. Most importantly, we view abilities and competencies both as being along a continuum rather than as being qualitatively distinct. Abilities are forms of developing competencies, and competencies are forms of developing expertise. Ultimately, we believe, these kinds of fusions will provide us with the kind of understanding of leadership (and other constructs) that will help people become the best leaders they can be. (Sternberg & Vroom, 2002, p. 314)

Relationship to Learner-Centered Leadership

One difference between the two approaches that Vroom notes is the difference between leadership development and training (his model) and leadership selection (Sternberg's model). Sternberg's leadership construct focuses on wisdom, intelligence, and creativity as attributes of a leader in the workplace. Sternberg's focus is on the leader as a person, and on the qualities or attributes deemed most significant to successful performances. Of the three qualities referenced, the wisdom attribute, doing wise things, resonates most closely with the change from "administration" to "leadership" and the focus on teaching and learning; it is based on valuing the learner, and balancing the interests of students, teachers, and administrators in reaching a common good.

CONCLUSION: PROMOTING DOCTORAL RESEARCH ON EDUCATIONAL LEADERSHIP

Richardson (2006) cites the Carnegie Foundation for the Advancement of Teaching to argue that education doctoral programs are intended to develop "stewards" of the field and enterprise of education. She argues that stewards "are able to generate new knowledge, understand the intellectual history of the field, use the best ideas and practices in current work, and represent that knowledge to others, both within and outside the field. Stewards have a respectful sense of the broader intellectual landscape, including paradigms, and questions, and they are able to speak about how their field contributes important understanding to these larger questions. They have a strong sense of obligation to their field and to helping preserve the best while promoting change and improvement" (Richardson, 2006, p. 251).

Richardson (2006) also suggests that the term *education* implies looking at the study of the field *and* the formal system that is being studied. In this sense education is a field of study, with implied theory and science and it is "an enterprise that consists of the various systems of education and therefore, primarily an activity" (p. 252). As such a doctoral program (PhD or EdD) is designed to prepare scholars who provide theory, research, and analysis of education settings, including the people who populate those settings.

The award winning research in this book has come out of the education doctoral programs and connects back to Senge's (1990) idea of leader as steward, one who is responsible for both the field of education study and for the education enterprise itself. In general, the award-winning research presented in this volume follow the traditions outlined in this chapter. More specifically, the research presented in this volume was selected based on the following criteria:

- alignment with the goals, mission, and purposes of the LTEL SIG;
- significance, uniqueness, and clarity of problem and its investigation;
- adequacy of conceptualization and development of research questions;
- quality of review of relevant theoretical and research literature;
- appropriateness and rigor of research design and methodology;
- quality and clarity of writing evidenced in the proposal summary and dissertation completion plan;
- quality of sponsor support;
- soundness of proposed dissertation completion timeline; and
- appropriate use of grant funds.

This brief framing of the research on educational leadership that is presented in this volume summarizes the evolution of the Learning and Teaching in Educational Leadership SIG as well as directions of research on educational leadership in the future. Some of the early research on leadership argued that principals were "instructional leaders," charged with leading other adults in ways that resulted in enhanced student learning. More recent research (Pont et al., 2008) points out that the school principal was second only to teachers, in fostering student learning. The movement away from management approaches to administering schools points to a greater emphasis on teaching and learning, and this view is now well established in the standards for administrator preparation (Educational Leadership Constituent Council) and expectations for on the job performance (Council of Chief State School Officers, 2008). These standards are embedded in the credentialing experiences of almost all graduate programs in school administration/educational leadership. Senge's (1990) view of "leader as steward" recognized new roles for leaders beyond that traditional management role. Spillane's (2006) work on distributed leadership makes clear that leadership is distributed across the organization, and for leadership to be fully understood, it must include those in formal leadership roles and well as those who exert influence behind the scenes. Ultimately, these views of leadership adopt more a systems perspective (Ackoff, 2010; Senge et al., 1999; Vickers, 1970), which expands what we know about leadership and how research contributes to an appreciation for the multiple ways that leadership exists in education settings.

REFERENCES

Ackoff, R. (2010). *Systems thinking for curious managers*. Axminister, Devon, UK: Triarchy Press.

American Psychological Association. (1997). *Learner-centered psychological principles: A framework for school redesign and reform*. Retrieved from http://www.apa.org/ed/lcp.html.

Barnard, C. (1968). Cambridge, MA: Harvard University Press. (Original work published 1938)

Bennis, W. (2003). *On becoming a leader* (Rev. ed.). Cambridge, MA: Perseus.

Council of Chief State School Officers. (2008). *Educational Leadership Policy Standards: ISLLC 2008*. Washington, DC: Authors.

Danzig, A. (2009, Spring). Learner-centered leadership versus learning-centered leadership: Small differences in words, large differences in meaning. *LTEL SIG Newsletter*, 1-2, 7-8, 14.

Danzig, A., Blankson, G., & Kiltz, G. (2007). A learner-centered approach to leadership preparation and professional development. In A. Danzig, K. Borman, B. Jones, & W. Wright (Eds.) *Learner-centered leadership: Research, policy, and practice* (pp. 51-72). Mahwah, NJ: Erlbaum.

Danzig, A., Borman, K., Jones, B., & Wright, W. (Eds.). (2007). *Learner-centered leadership: Research, policy, and practice*. Mahwah, NJ: Erlbaum.

Dewey, J. (1916). *Democracy and education*. New York, NY: Macmillan

Elmore, R. (2008). Leadership as the practice of improvement. In B. Pont, D. Nusche, & D. Hopkins (Eds.), *Improving school leadership: Vol. 2. Case studies on system leadership* (pp. 37-67). Paris, France: Organisation for Economic Co-operation and Development.

Freire, P. (1970). *Pedagogy of the oppressed*. New York, NY: Penguin.

Gonzalez, N., Moll, L., & Amanti, C. (2005). *Funds of knowledge: Theorizing practices in households, communities, and classrooms*. Mahwah, NJ: Lawrence Erlbaum.

Greenleaf, R. (1991). *Servant leadership: A journey into the nature of legitimate power and greatness*. New York, NY: Paulist Press. (Original work published 1977)

Heifetz, R. (1994). *Leadership without easy answers*. Cambridge, MA: Harvard University Press.

Hess, F., & Kelly, A. (2005). Learning to lead? What gets taught in principal preparation programs. Retrieved from http://www.hks.harvard.edu/pepg/PDF/Papers/Hess_Kelly_Learning_to_Lead_PEPG05.02.pdf

Levine, A. (2005). *Educating school leaders*. New York, NY: Teachers College, The Education Schools Project.

Lieberman, A., Falk, B., & Alexander, A. (1995). *A culture in the making: Leadership in learner-centered schools*. In K. Rehage, J. Oakes, & K. H. Quartz, Creating New Educational Communities. National Society for the Study of Education, University of Chicago Press.

Lieberman, A., Falk, B., & Alexander, A. (2007). A culture in the making: Leadership in learner-centered schools. Revised and Updated. In A. Danzig, K. Borman, B. Jones, & W. Wright, *Learner-centered leadership: Research, policy, and practice* (pp. 23-499). Mahwah, NJ: Erlbaum.

National Research Council. (2000). *How people learn: Brain, mind, experience, and school: Expanded edition*. Washington, DC: National Academy Press.

Polanyi, M. (1962). *Personal knowledge*. Chicago, IL: University of Chicago Press.

Polanyi, M. (1967). *Tacit knowledge*. Garden City, NY: Anchor Books.

Pont, B., Nusche, D., & Hopkins, D. (Eds.). (2008). *Improving school leadership: Vol. 1. Policy and practice*. Paris, France: Organisation for Economic Co-operation and Development.

Putnam, R. (1991). Recipes and reflective learning: "What would prevent you from saying it that way?" In D. Schon (Eds.), *The reflective turn: Case studies in and on education practice* (pp. 145-163). New York, NY: Teachers College Press.

Richardson, V. (2006). Stewards of a field, stewards of an enterprise: The doctorate in education. In C. Golde, G. Walker, & Associates (Eds.), *Envisioning the future of doctoral education: Preparing stewards of the discipline Carnegie essays on the doctorate* (pp. 251-267). San Francisco, CA: Jossey-Bass.

Robinson, V. (2011). *Student-centered leadership*. San Francisco, CA: John Wiley & Sons.

Schön, D. (1991). *The reflective turn*. Boston, MA: Harvard University press.

Senge, P. (1990, Fall). The leader's new work: Building learning organizations. *Sloan Management Review*, 7-23.

Senge, P., Kleiner, A., Roberts, C., Ross, R., Roth, G., & Smith, B. (1999). *The dance of change: The challenges to sustaining momentum in learning organizations*. New York, NY: Currency/Doubleday.

Sergiovanni, T. (2001). *The principalship: A reflective practice perspective* (4th ed.). Boston, MA: Allyn & Bacon

Spillane, J. (2006). *Distributed leadership*. San Francisco, CA: Jossey-Bass.

Starrett, R. J. (2007). Moral issues in a test-driven accountability agenda: Moral challenges for learning centered leadership. In A. Danzig, K. Borman, B. Jones, & W. Wright (Eds.), *Learner-centered leadership* (pp. 275-290). Mahwah, NJ: Erlbaum.

Sternberg, R., & Vroom, V. (2002). Theoretical letters. The person versus the situation in leadership. *Leadership Quarterly, 13*, 301-323.

Terry, R. (1993). *Authentic leadership: Courage in action*. San Francisco, CA: Jossey-Bass.

Vickers, G. (1995). *The art of judgment: A study of policy making*. Thousand Oaks, CA: SAGE.

CHAPTER 2

PERCEPTIONS OF ILLINOIS SCHOOL DISTRICT SUPERINTENDENTS REGARDING THE EFFICACY OF THEIR SUPERINTENDENT PREPARATION

Arthur J. Fessler and Donald G. Hackmann

ABSTRACT

This quantitative study, using survey research methods, examined whether Illinois public school superintendents perceived that their superintendent preparation programs adequately prepared them for the superintendency. The study examined superintendents' perceptions about the relevance of six educational leadership standards for central office administration, noting whether these standards were embedded in university-based leadership preparation programs, as well as the importance of these standards to their administrative practice. An online questionnaire was administered to the 868 Illinois school district superintendents who held their appointments during the 2009-2010 school year; 314 responses were received for a 36.2% response rate.

Findings revealed that more than three fourths of superintendents were satisfied with the training they received from their preparation programs. Respondents reported that their training provided a moderate degree of

Research in Learning and Teaching in Educational Leadership
pp. 17–53

alignment to the leadership standards. Respondents recommended the following changes to strengthen superintendent preparation programs: (a) more focus on hands-on and practical experiences, such as internships; (b) more emphasis on fiscal, finance, and budget issues; (c) increased use of instructors who were current, successful superintendents; (d) additional content related to politics and political culture; (e) development of mentor programs; and (f) content related to building positive relationships with school boards.

Findings also revealed a need to more fully incorporate leadership standards in superintendent preparation program design. The mean emphasis ratings were lower than the mean importance ratings across all 39 leadership items within the six standards, indicating that superintendent preparation programs were not fully addressing these standards within their curricula. Although there were no differences in mean emphasis ratings of the six standards within the preparation programs based upon gender, female superintendents rated the importance of all six leadership standards higher than did male superintendents. Additionally, respondents noted that a focus on instructional leadership was largely missing in most preparation programs, reporting that only 38% of the questionnaire items addressing instructional leadership practices were emphasized or highly emphasized in their superintendent training. Yet, recognizing the importance of their roles as learning leaders of their school districts, respondents reported that 87% of the items linked to instructional leadership were important or highly important to their practice.

The public school district superintendency has changed significantly over the past few decades (Brunner, Grogan, & Björk, 2002; Murphy, 2003), evolving into a highly challenging position that is fraught with complex issues, accountability for student achievement, difficulties in managing competing priorities, a necessity to negotiate through conflicts, and the need to facilitate continuous district reforms. School district leaders are charged with a variety of responsibilities, including being competent fiscal managers, politically savvy leaders who maintain effective relationships with their school boards and community constituents, and learning leaders who are dedicated to enhanced learning of every student in their district. Although numerous factors have contributed to the changing nature of the superintendency, initiatives such as No Child Left Behind mandates, the Common Core State Standards, the Race to the Top competition, and changing teacher and administrator evaluation expectations have added an unprecedented element of accountability for increased student achievement. Due to these increasingly complex job demands, numerous scholars (Cooper, Fusarelli, Jackson, & Poster, 2002; Grogan & Andrews, 2002; Levine, 2005; Waters & Marzano, 2006) have questioned whether superintendents possess the essential knowledge and skills for their myriad responsibilities.

In recent years, critics have asserted that superintendent training lacks rigor and fails to provide the requisite training to adequately prepare public school district superintendents for their roles (Cambron-McCabe & Cunningham, 2002; Levine, 2005). Some have claimed that superintendents have a low regard for the quality of their administrator preparation (Grogan & Andrews, 2002), but in national surveys that have been conducted throughout the past few decades, school superintendents have provided favorable ratings of the overall quality of their university-based preparation programs (Cunningham & Hentages, 1982; Glass, Björk, & Brunner, 2000; Kowalski, McCord, Petersen, Young, & Ellerson, 2011). There appears to be a disconnect between the assertions of critics and the beliefs of practicing superintendents regarding the effectiveness of superintendent preparation programs in colleges and universities across the United States. Because superintendents are the recipients of this training and the quality of the leadership preparation curriculum influences their effectiveness in their administrative roles, further investigation into superintendents' perceptions of superintendent preparation quality is warranted.

School district superintendents typically obtain their training through university-based leadership preparation programs, and both critics and supporters of these programs have conceded that many of the nation's programs are in need of revision (Cooper et al., 2002; Darling-Hammond, LaPointe, Meyerson, Orr, & Cohen, 2007; Levine, 2005; Waters & Marzano, 2006). Some have argued that universal leadership standards, such as the Interstate School Leaders Licensure Consortium standards that were developed in 1996 and later revised in 2008 (Council of Chief State School Officers [CCSSO], 1996, 2008), could serve as a mechanism to strengthen the curriculum, increase rigor in course experiences and experiential activities, and guide the restructuring of state licensure and superintendent preparation regulations (Murphy, 2003; Wilmore, 2008). Although numerous studies have been conducted on leadership preparation program quality, the majority of this research has focused on principal preparation programming, and the preparation of central office administrators has been virtually ignored (Cooper et al., 2002). Analyzing over 2,000 articles on leadership preparation published between 1975 and 2002, Murphy and Vriesenga (2004) concluded that fewer than 3% of these publications involved empirical research and only a small proportion focused on the superintendency. In fact, according to Cooper et al. (2002), many assertions about superintendent preparation program quality involve generalizations gleaned from research on principal preparation programming. Clearly, there is a need to fill the gap in the literature and to examine programs that prepare aspiring superintendents.

This chapter begins with a brief overview of research on the superintendency and superintendent preparation programming. Next, findings from a dissertation study examining Illinois public school district superintendents' perceptions of the adequacy of their leadership training are presented. In the discussion/implications section, comparisons are made to previous research, and recommendations are provided for school districts, policymakers and professional organizations, and higher education institutions with leadership preparation programs.

REVIEW OF RESEARCH ON THE SUPERINTENDENCY AND SUPERINTENDENT PREPARATION

Since the publication of *A Nation at Risk* in the early 1980s (National Commission on Excellence in Education, 1983) and the enactment of the No Child Left Behind legislation in 2002, school districts and their educational leaders have been condemned for a lack of direction and unsatisfactory global student outcomes. Educational leaders have been criticized for being unable to keep pace with continuing societal changes and the inability to meet the educational needs of their students and communities (Glasman & Glasman, 1997). Superintendents must possess a variety of skills in order to lead their districts successfully, and with the growing emphasis on accountability for student achievement, providing quality leadership for student learning arguably is paramount among these skills (Copland & Knapp, 2006; Knapp, Copland, & Talbert, 2003). Although this model includes aspects of the political and managerial roles that are inherent in the superintendency, leadership behaviors that are centered on student learning are central focus of this approach. This section begins with a brief overview of leadership for student learning (Copland & Knapp, 2006; Knapp et al., 2003), which was employed as a theoretical framework to guide this study.

Leadership for Learning

Leadership for learning has been conceptualized as a model that supports the superintendent's efforts that focus on the development of a learning-focused culture throughout the school district organization (Copland & Knapp, 2006). The primary emphasis of this approach is to build collective trust among stakeholders, create a vision, and develop relationships in which principals, teachers, parents, and students share values, goals, and beliefs. School superintendents who skillfully implement leadership for learning strategies create resilient systems that evidence shared leadership, collaborative cultures, and continuous learners throughout the entire organization. A leadership for learning approach enables superintendents to create powerful, equitable learning opportunities for students, professionals, and the school system as a learning organization (Copland & Knapp, 2006; Knapp et al., 2003).

Instructionally focused superintendents are integral actors in district-level actions that focus on student learning (Copland & Knapp, 2006; Leithwood, Louis, Anderson, & Wahlstrom, 2004). Leithwood et al. (2004) concluded that successful leadership can play a significant role in improving student learning, noting that effective leadership behaviors are essential to the successful implementation of large-scale reforms. Leithwood et al. maintained that both building- and district-level leaders provide a critical bridge between the implementation of educational reform initiatives and their learning consequences for students. In addition, effective leadership has the greatest influence in circumstances in which it is most needed—in those schools with the lowest levels of academic performance.

Superintendent Licensure, Standards, and Preparation

Each of the 50 states has responsibility for the oversight and regulation of its school districts and educational personnel; consequently, regulations for administrative licensure and for university-based superintendent preparation programs are determined by each individual state (Cooper et al., 2002). State statutes and administrative rules, which provide specifications for administrative licensure and regulations for leadership preparation programming, must be attentive to the increasing complexity of the superintendency as well as sufficiently flexible to address changing demands on individuals in this role (Kowalski & Brunner, 2011). Regulation of the superintendency has been contentious since the inception of the position (Callahan, 1966); concerns related to training and licensure accelerated in the 1980s and continued to gain momentum at the turn of the 21st century as a result of accelerating educational reforms. Some have argued that changes such as the elimination of ineffective training programs, development of a national curriculum for the preparation of school principals and superintendents, adoption of leadership standards for licensure, and training that focuses on student learning would produce higher quality professional preparation and improve the licensure process (Björk & Kowalski, 2005). Additionally, some critics outside the professoriate have advocated for the complete deregulation of existing administrative licensure requirements for principals and superintendents

(Broad Foundation and Thomas B. Fordham Institute, 2003; Hess, 2003). According to Petersen, Fusarelli, and Kowalski (2008), as of 2008, several states no longer required a license for the superintendency or had developed state statutes providing alternative routes to administrative licensure. In 2010, while approximately 85% of superintendents nationwide had earned their licensure through an accredited university-based preparation program (Kowalski et al., 2011), approximately one third of superintendents of urban school districts (enrollments of 25,000 students or more) had obtained an alternative license, and nearly 14% did not hold a valid state superintendent license (Kowalski et al., 2001). The state of Illinois, which was the focus of this study, does require aspiring superintendents to complete a superintendent preparation program and to obtain a superintendent's endorsement, with the exception of the Chicago Public Schools system, the third largest school system in the nation.

Numerous professional associations and task forces have developed leadership standards through the years in an attempt to guide leadership practice, preparation, and licensure for school superintendents. The origin of leadership standards lies with the American Association of School Administrators (AASA) *Guidelines for the Preparation of School Administrators* developed in 1979. The National Policy Board for Educational Administration (NPBEA), a consortium of professional associations in educational leadership and policy, initiated the standards movement in 1989 with the publication of standards for the principalship. In 1993, AASA published a listing of eight standards for the superintendency. The work of AASA and NPBEA paved the way for the formation of the Interstate School Leaders Licensure Consortium (ISLLC), and a working group consisting of members of administrator organizations and university faculty members developed six research-based standards for educational leaders in 1996 (CCSSO, 1996) that subsequently were revised in 2008 (CCSSO, 2008). The ISLLC standards have been further developed into standards for building-level and central office administrators through the Educational Leadership Constituent Council (ELCC) standards, which are used by leadership preparation programs to attain accreditation of their principal and superintendent preparation programs (NPBEA, 2009). In addition, Waters and Marzano (2006) developed six sets of leadership behaviors that have a positive correlation with student and district outcomes.

Despite some disagreement regarding which leadership standards or behaviors should be identified to guide the professional preparation of aspiring superintendents (Hoyle, 2004), standards and leadership preparation remain an integral part of national educational policy discourse (Levine, 2005; Murphy, 2003; Waters & Marzano, 2006). Inherent in this dialogue is an affirmation that the roles and responsibilities of the school superintendent and school principal are unique; therefore, because these administrative positions are distinct, preparation programs should provide separate training experiences to reflect these differences. There is consensus among many researchers (Hess & Kelly, 2007; Levine, 2005; Orr & Pounder, 2006; Young & Kochan, 2004) that reform must occur in superintendent preparation programs in order to keep pace with changes in role expectations for the superintendency, and the literature builds a compelling case for leadership training that stresses leading for learning as a core component (Orr & Pounder, 2006; Young & Kochan, 2004). Yet, scholars have acknowledged that curricular reforms have begun to occur in leadership preparation programs, spurred in part by the incorporation of the ISLLC standards into state requirements for administrator preparation (Glass & Franceschini 2007; Hackmann & McCarthy, 2011).

Some critics have suggested that the leadership preparation curriculum in most universities is not coherent but consists of a series of unrelated courses designed to meet state accreditation requirements that were promulgated several decades ago (Hoyle, Björk, Collier, & Glass, 2005; Levine, 2005). Many educational leadership professors have explained that there is a lack of clarity regarding specific elements that should be included in this reform (Orr & Pounder, 2006; Young & Kochan, 2004). For example, superintendent preparation in some institutions is considered deficient because it is perceived as being merely an extension of principalship curriculum (Cooper et al., 2004), or advanced coursework is provided to superintendents that does not address their professional needs. Grogan and Andrews (2002) observed that "few universities have programs tailored specifically for the superintendent position, although most PhD and EdD programs in educational administration are considered to be preparation programs for superintendents" (p. 245). Pointing out that it is not the "how" but the "what," Kowalski (2003) suggested that the most important component of training is the curriculum, which highlights the importance of creating coursework and learning activities that reflect the unique responsibilities of school superintendents. Unfortunately, there is relatively little empirical evidence to support features of effective programming.

One recurring theme is the deficiencies in practical clinical experiences that need to be embedded in superintendent preparation. Fry, Bottoms, O'Neill, and Walker (2007) stressed that administrative preparation programs must be held accountable for relevant content and the implementation of quality school-based internships. These researchers suggested that many field-based experiences are experiences in name only and fail to ensure that the student is immersed in a rich and meaningful clinical experience. In short, these critics assert that superintendent training often is steeped in theory and does not adequately provide students with theory-to-practice connections so that they have, real-world, field-based opportunities to learn their craft. In today's high-stakes era of improved student achievement, it is necessary for school district leadership to acquire the skills from adequately designed programs that provide them with the technical skills to facilitate improved student learning gains within their districts. Fry et al. (2007) encouraged programs to create meaningful and sustained clinical internships that expose aspiring superintendents to problems of practice that occur throughout a continuous 12-month period, so that these individuals have a more comprehensive understanding of leadership issues that arise at varying points of the academic year. In addition, in a position paper prepared to recommend reforms in leader preparation in the state of Illinois, the Commission on School Leader Preparation in Illinois Colleges and Universities (2006) emphasized the importance of strengthening partnerships between university programs and school districts. Commission members asserted that this enhanced relationship would address claims that university-based programs are irrelevant and out of touch with educational needs and also provide opportunities for future leaders to experience relevant on-site training in school settings. Levine (2005) concurred and reported that preparation programs "offered little in the way of meaningful clinical or field based experiences" (p. 41).

Research on the Superintendency

The AASA has conducted the most prominent survey research studies of the superintendency in the United States, publishing state of the superintendency reports every decade since the 1920s that have described the perceptions of these administrators regarding the expectations of their positions and the quality of their leadership preparation. The 2000 report (Glass et al., 2000), which involved 2,262 superintendents, found that two thirds of respondents rated the quality of their preparation programs as *good*. Respondents identified the following weaknesses in their training: (a) lack of hands-on application, (b) inadequate access to technology, (c) failure to link content to practice, and (d) too much emphasis placed on professors' personal experiences (Glass et al., 2000). Glass et al. (2000) concluded that the 21st century school superintendent must spend significant time working with community groups, responding to state and federal mandates, and working with the public in the area of vouchers, home schooling, and privatization. The authors contended that the successful school superintendent must have "excellent communication skills, understand the instructional process, and work to create functional coalitions that will ensure financial and educational survival of the public school system" (p. 13).

The most recent AASA study conducted in 2010, with responses from nearly 2,000 superintendents across the United States, yielded interesting results regarding the changing demographics of individuals employed in the superintendency as well as the changing duties inherent in this position. Kowalski et al. (2011) noted that the responsibilities of the superintendency have grown to encompass not only student achievement but also the ongoing diversification of student and faculty/staff populations; advancements in technology; increasing expectations from state and federal governments, the school board, and community; and the increasing globalization of society. They also observed that the superintendency has become increasingly diverse, with 24.1% of respondents being female, compared to 13.2% in 2000 (Glass et al., 2000), and 6% persons of color. Only a slight majority of the respondents (50.8%) reported that they intended to remain in the superintendency in the year 2015, indicating the potential for significant turnover in this central office position within a relatively short period of time. Nearly 8 in 10 respondents (78.7%) rated their academic preparation for the superintendency as *good* or *excellent* (Kowalski et al., 2011); there were no differences in ratings of the quality of academic preparation when analyzed by race/ethnicity or gender.

Kowalski et al. (2011) reported that advances in technology and the use of social media have raised the expectations for regular communication among key stakeholders and the community. Another factor mentioned was increasing pressure linked to mandates of state and federal government and ongoing educational reforms. According to Kowalski et al., the majority of respondents perceived that the No Child Left Behind legislation is more of a liability than an asset. Further, superintendents were struggling to stretch their already scarce resources to hire and retain excellent teachers and administrators and to provide quality educational experiences for students—in effect, doing more with less.

Using the 1996 ISLLC standards as the framework for his survey research, Barnett (2004) examined the professional practices of over 2,000 principals, supervisors, and superintendents, as well as their feelings of preparedness upon completion of their preparation programs. Respondents were asked to determine the frequency in which they practiced the standards and then rate the effectiveness of their graduate programs in preparing aspiring administrators for each identified standard. In all cases, frequency of completing the task was greater than the effectiveness of the preparation for particular responsibilities. Respondents recognized that the standards were in line with the daily activities of the leader but not necessarily were fully integrated as a component in their courses and programmatic experiences. The study yielded mixed reviews, with school leaders expressing satisfaction with some areas of training and dissatisfaction with other areas.

Petersen et al. (2008) conducted a quantitative study of novice superintendent perceptions of preparation adequacy and problems of practice. The study included superintendents in four states (California, Missouri, North Carolina, and Ohio) who began their appointments at the start of the 2005-2006 school year. Of the 200 novice superintendents identified for the study, 118 completed the survey instrument, a 59% response rate. Findings revealed that respondents felt adequately prepared and were generally positive about their preparation programs, although they reported that they could have more extensive training in school finance, school law, and school board relations.

This review of literature provides some insights into research on the superintendency and also concerns about the adequacy of university-based superintendency programming. Although some research indicates that superintendents generally report being satisfied with the quality of their training, a more comprehensive investigation of superintendents' perceptions of their preparation programming could be helpful in guiding educational leadership faculty members' development of the superintendency curriculum in their institutions.

RESEARCH QUESTIONS AND METHODS

This quantitative study utilized survey research methods, through the use of an online questionnaire, to examine the perceptions of Illinois school district superintendents regarding the effectiveness of their superintendent training. The following research questions were addressed:

1. Did superintendents perceive their superintendent preparation was effective in preparing them for their positions, and to what extent did their training emphasize the content of the leadership standards?

2. To what extent do superintendents perceive that leadership standards are important to their professional practice?

3. Do superintendents who received their superintendent endorsements after No Child Left Behind (NCLB) implementation place more emphasis on the content of the leadership standards than those trained prior to NCLB implementation?

4. To what extent are superintendents' perceptions about the emphasis on leadership standards in preparation programs related to their perceptions of the importance of these standards when performing their duties?

5. What changes do superintendents recommend to superintendent preparation programming?

The survey instrument incorporated items from the ISLLC leadership standards that were revised in 2008 (CCSSO, 2008), the ELCC standards for school district leaders (NPBEA, 2009), and the effective superintendent leadership responsibilities and practices identified by Waters and Marzano (2006). A matrix was developed that contained all indicators of these three resources; common descriptors were identified and redundancies were eliminated, resulting in 39 items contained within the six standards. Although the six standards closely resembled the six ISLLC school leadership standards, the 39 functions contained within the standards were carefully constructed to be representative of school leadership practices at the school district level. The questionnaire also included two open-ended questions to solicit feedback from participants concerning their recommendations to improve superintendent preparation program quality.

To ensure content validity, an initial draft of the questionnaire was shared with five professors in U.S. higher education institutions who engage in superintendency research, and their feedback was incorporated into a revised questionnaire. As a final step, a cognitive laboratory was conducted (Fowler, 2009) with five assistant superintendents in Illinois public school districts. These individuals identified items that lacked clarity or were redundant, suggested revisions, and provided input regarding the overall length of the questionnaire and estimated time for completion; this commentary also was assimilated into the revised instrument.

All public school district superintendents in Illinois (the chief executive officer of the Chicago Public Schools was excluded, because he does not operate as a district superintendent) were sent an electronic mailing, inviting them to complete the online questionnaire. A total of 314 of the 868 district superintendents responded, for a 36.2% response rate. Table 2.1 provides a demographic overview of the respondents. The typical respondent was a White male, 50-59 years of age, with a doctoral degree, employed at the elementary district level, hired as superintendent prior to the implementation of NCLB, and having completed a superintendent program at a comprehensive university. Of those respondents providing their gender and race/ethnicity, 28.0% were females and 2.6% were persons of color. Compared with the 2010 AASA national superintendent study (Kowalski et al., 2011), a slightly higher proportion of respondents to this Illinois study were female and a smaller percentage were persons of color.

SPSS (version 17.0) was used for quantitative analysis; inferential tests included independent and paired samples *t* tests, analysis of variance, and

Table 2.1. Demographic Profile of Respondents

Category	Frequency	Percent
Age		
30-39	17	5.4
40-49	71	22.6
50-59	133	42.4
60+	44	14.0
No response	49	15.6
Gender		
Female	74	23.6
Male	190	60.5
No response	50	15.9
Race		
White	259	82.5
Other	7	2.2
No response	48	15.3
Highest degree earned		
Master's	6	1.9
Educational specialist	114	36.3
Juris doctorate	3	1.0
Doctor of education	100	31.8
Doctor of philosophy	41	13.1
No response	50	15.9
Type of district		
Unit (PK-12)	105	33.4
Elementary (PK-8)	129	41.1
High school (9-12)	29	9.2
No response	51	16.2
Superintendent preparation completion based upon NCLB enactment		
Training completed pre-NCLB	143	45.5
Training completed post-NCLB	114	36.3
No response	57	18.2
Institution type from which superintendent preparation was attained		
Research	111	35.4
Doctoral	30	9.6
Comprehensive	121	38.5
No response	52	16.6

**Table 2.2.   Reliability Results for Emphasis
and Importance Ratings Using Cronbach's Alpha**

Standard	n	Items	t
Emphasis in superintendent preparation program			
Standard 1: Shared vision of learning	308	6	0.902
Standard 2: School culture and instructional program	282	10	0.896
Standard 3: Organizational management	270	8	0.879
Standard 4: Collaboration with families and community	270	5	0.907
Standard 5: Ethical behaviors	268	6	0.885
Standard 6: Political, social, economic, legal, cultural context	265	4	0.815
Importance to administrative practice			
Standard 1: Shared vision of learning	305	6	0.843
Standard 2: School culture and instructional program	275	10	0.862
Standard 3: Organizational management	275	8	0.826
Standard 4: Collaboration with families and community	271	5	0.848
Standard 5: Ethical behaviors	264	6	0.860
Standard 6: Political, social, economic, legal, cultural context	265	4	0.757

Pearson correlation. Analyses were conducted for respondent subgroups, based upon respondent gender, age, years of superintendency experience, type of school district (elementary [K-8], high school [9-12], or unit [Pk-12]), when the superintendent licensure was obtained (prior to or after NCLB implementation), and type of institution from which superintendent training was completed. Institutions were categorized into three types—research, doctoral, and comprehensive, through combining the Carnegie Foundation for the Advancement of Teaching (n.d.) basic classifications. For this study, research universities included doctorate-granting universities with very high research activity (RU/VH) and high research activity (RU/H), doctoral universities included those classified as doctoral/research universities (DRU), and the remaining category, comprehensive, included all other institution types that were reported as a lower tier of research activity.

Reliability was assessed by computing Cronbach's alpha on the emphasis and importance ratings of the six standards. All scales yielded good to excellent internal reliability, with Cronbach's alpha coefficients ranging between .757 and .907 (Table 2.2).

FINDINGS

This section contains the findings of the study, presented by the topics of the five research questions. Results also are presented when significant differences were identified for respondent subgroups.

Preparation for the Superintendency and Emphasis of Leadership Standards

Using a 5-point scale (1 = *very ineffective*, 5 = *very effective*), respondents rated the extent to which their university-based superintendent preparation programs were effective in preparing them to fulfill the responsibilities of their positions. Over three fourths (78%) of respondents reported that their university-based training was effective, having rated their programs as either *very effective* or *somewhat effective*.

Using a 5-point scale (1 = *no emphasis*, 5 = *extensive emphasis*), respondents also rated the extent to which their superintendent preparation programs had placed an emphasis on the 39 central office leadership functions contained within the six standards. The ratings for indicators contained within each standard were combined and averaged, thus enabling the calculation of an overall mean rating for each of the six standards. As noted in Table 2.3, respondents perceived that their preparation programs placed only *moderate emphasis* on the content contained within the standards of shared vision of learning ($M = 3.06$); school culture and instructional program ($M = 3.12$); organizational management ($M = 3.18$); collaboration with families and community ($M = 2.96$); ethical behaviors ($M = 3.08$); and political, social, economic, legal, and cultural context ($M = 3.28$) (Table 2.3).

An inspection of the descriptive results indicated that all distributions were relatively normal for the six emphasis dependent variables and that the respondents' perceptions were diverse. Therefore, it was possible to test for the presence of significant differences and significant relationships because the data yielded a sufficient degree of variability. Comparing the mean emphasis ratings of the content of the six standards by gender, females and males generally provided comparable ratings, although females reported a more extensive emphasis of shared vision of learning and ethical behaviors in their programs than did males, and males reported that the organizational management standard was more fully emphasized in their programs than did females (Table 2.4). Independent samples t tests, however, found no significant differences on any of the six standards based upon gender (Table 2.5), indicating that both

Table 2.3. Emphasis and Importance Ratings for Functions Within Standards

Item	Emphasis		Importance		Difference Between Importance and Emphasis
	Mean	SD	Mean	SD	
Standard 1: Shared vision of learning					
• Utilizing a collaborative approach to develop the district vision and mission	3.06	0.86	4.17	0.59	1.11
	3.24	0.98	4.07	0.87	0.83
• Developing and adopting districtwide, research-based instructional goals in collaboration with school board members and principals	2.87	0.99	4.14	0.79	1.27
• Developing and implementing a district improvement plan that addresses operations and student achievement	2.85	1.06	4.29	0.74	1.44
• Including principals and school board members in the development of the district improvement plan	2.94	1.10	4.11	0.80	1.17
• Engaging in continuous and sustained improvement though professional learning and transformational change	3.50	1.08	4.19	0.78	0.69
• Developing strategies for monitoring and evaluating the district instructional plan	2.96	1.08	4.21	0.76	1.25
Standard 2: School culture and instructional program	3.12	0.74	4.26	0.45	1.14
• Developing a culture of collaboration, trust, learning, and high expectations that ensures student success	3.43	1.02	4.45	0.65	1.02
• Maintaining Board support for district goals for achievement and instruction	3.09	1.12	4.42	0.64	1.33
• Developing quality curriculum, including principles/theories of learning, appropriate instructional techniques, and monitoring and evaluating instruction	3.32	1.00	4.20	0.69	0.88
• Creating a personalized and motivating learning environment for students	2.87	1.07	4.04	0.77	1.17
• Supervising staff performance for high quality teacher, principal, and district practice	3.60	0.97	4.46	0.62	0.86
• Developing methods of evaluation, accountability systems, data collection, and analysis of data to monitor student progress	2.99	1.12	4.40	0.67	1.41
• Allocating resources for quality professional development of teachers and principals to achieve district goals in order to improve teaching and learning	2.98	0.99	4.13	0.73	1.15

(Table continues on next page)

Table 2.3. (Continued)

Item	Emphasis		Importance		Difference Between Importance and Emphasis
	Mean	SD	Mean	SD	
Standard 2 (Continued)					
• Creating district systems that promote efficient practices in the management of all resources	3.02	0.96	4.11	0.70	1.09
• Promoting the use of technologies to support effective teaching and learning	2.69	1.11	4.05	0.72	1.36
• Monitoring and evaluating the impact of the instructional program	3.24	0.98	4.36	0.64	1.12
Standard 3: Organizational management					
• Assessing and managing organizational, operational, and legal resources of the district	3.18	0.72	4.14	0.49	0.96
• Strategically aligning fiscal and educational resources throughout the district	3.50	0.92	4.18	0.72	0.68
• Efficiently utilizing human, fiscal, and technological resources, including maintaining facilities	3.21	0.99	4.39	0.66	1.18
• Developing strategies for providing a safe and secure district environment, including a substance-, weapon-, and violence-free work environment	3.08	0.95	4.12	0.72	1.04
• Developing and sustaining the capacity for distributed leadership throughout the organization	2.67	1.08	4.01	0.75	1.34
• Providing autonomy to principals to lead their schools, with expectations for alignment of district goals and use of resources for professional development	3.33	1.00	4.07	0.76	0.74
• Managing personal managerial and leadership responsibilities	3.20	0.99	4.10	0.74	0.90
	3.37	0.97	4.06	0.71	0.69
• Ensuring teacher and organizational time is focused to support quality instruction and student learning	3.07	0.96	4.18	0.71	1.11
Standard 4: Collaboration with families and communities					
• Collecting and analyzing data and information from the community that is pertinent to the district	2.96	0.86	3.90	0.62	0.94
• Promoting understanding, appreciation, and use of the community's diverse cultural, social, and intellectual resources	2.93	0.96	3.85	0.77	0.92
	2.95	0.99	3.71	0.84	0.76

• Building and sustaining positive relationships with families and caregivers that meets their needs	2.93	1.03	3.94	0.79	1.01
• Developing strategies for on-going effective oral and written communication with families and caregivers	2.89	1.03	3.94	0.74	1.05
• Building and sustaining productive relationships with community partners	3.10	1.04	4.05	0.76	0.95
Standard 5: Ethical behavior	3.08	0.85	3.91	0.65	0.83
• Ensuring a system of accountability for every student's academic and social success	2.88	1.01	4.20	0.75	1.32
• Utilizing federal, state, and local legal/policy guidance to create operational definitions of accountability, equity, and social justice	3.00	1.05	3.77	0.86	0.77
• Understanding the impact of self-awareness, reflective practice, transparency, and ethical behavior on leadership	3.36	1.13	4.15	0.82	0.79
• Safeguarding the values of democracy, equity, and diversity	3.03	1.10	3.81	0.90	0.78
• Understanding current ethical and moral issues facing education, government, and business and their consequences	3.26	1.03	3.96	0.82	0.70
• Understanding and promoting the relationship between social justice, district culture, and student achievement	2.92	1.05	3.60	0.90	0.68
Standard 6: Political, social, economic, legal, cultural context	3.28	0.83	4.03	0.59	0.75
• Understanding the policies, laws, and regulations enacted by local, state, and federal authorities that affect school districts	3.73	0.94	4.29	0.72	0.56
• Advocating for children, families, and caregivers	2.96	1.05	3.86	0.85	0.90
• Understanding the larger political, social, economic, legal and cultural contexts and how they affect student learning	3.37	1.03	3.96	0.76	0.59
• Utilizing power and political skills to influence local, state, and federal decisions affecting student learning	3.05	1.08	4.02	0.79	0.97

Table 2.4.   Mean Emphasis Scores on Standards by Gender

				95% CI	
Emphasis	*n*	*Mean*	*SD*	*Lower*	*Upper*
Standard 1: Shared vision of learning					
Females	74	3.13	0.84	2.94	3.32
Males	190	2.96	0.86	2.84	3.08
Standard 2: School culture and instructional program					
Females	74	3.07	0.77	2.89	3.25
Males	190	3.10	0.75	2.99	3.21
Standard 3: Organizational management					
Females	73	3.11	0.77	2.93	3.29
Males	189	3.18	0.71	3.08	3.28
Standard 4: Collaboration with families and community					
Females	74	2.96	0.86	2.76	3.15
Males	189	2.95	0.87	2.83	3.07
Standard 5: Ethical behavior					
Females	74	3.22	0.90	3.01	3.42
Males	188	3.01	0.82	2.90	3.13
Standard 6: Political, social, economic, legal, cultural context					
Females	74	3.28	0.87	3.08	3.48
Males	189	3.27	0.81	3.15	3.38

**Table 2.5.   Independent Sample *t* Test Results:
Mean Emphasis Scores on Standards by Gender**

				95% CI	
Emphasis	*t*	*df*	*p*	*Lower*	*Upper*
Standard 1: Shared vision of learning	1.48	262	0.141	−0.06	0.40
Standard 2: School culture and instructional program	−0.30	262	0.763	−0.24	0.17
Standard 3: Organizational management	−0.67	260	0.501	−0.26	0.13
Standard 4: Collaboration with families and community	0.07	261	0.947	−0.23	0.24
Standard 5: Ethical behaviors	1.76	260	0.079	−0.02	0.43
Standard 6: Political, social, economic, legal, cultural	0.12	261	0.904	−0.21	0.24

males and females held similar perceptions of the content contained in their superintendency programs.

In addition, no significant differences were found, based upon the type of higher education institution from which respondents earned their superintendent endorsement, respondent age, or the type of Illinois school district. However, there was a relationship between highest degree earned, year endorsement was received, years of experience, and emphasis ratings. Highest degree earned was negatively correlated to the emphasis scores for shared vision of learning, school culture and instructional program, and collaboration with families and communities. Year that endorsement was received was positively correlated to the emphasis scores for shared vision of learning; school culture and instructional program; collaboration with family and community; ethical behaviors; and political, social, economic, legal, and cultural context. Finally, years of superintendency experience was negatively correlated to the emphasis scores for shared vision of learning and ethical behaviors.

Importance of Leadership Standards to Superintendent Practice

Respondents rated the extent to which the leadership standards were important to their daily administrative practices as public school superintendents, using a 5-point scale (1 = *no importance*, 5 = *extensive importance*). The respondents perceived that the six standards were of *moderate* to *high importance*, as follows: shared vision of learning ($M = 4.17$); school culture and instructional program ($M = 4.26$); organizational management ($M = 4.14$); collaboration with families and community ($M = 3.90$); ethical behaviors ($M = 3.91$); and political, social, economic, legal, and cultural context ($M = 4.03$) (Table 2.3). Standards related to teaching and learning (shared vision of learning; school culture and instructional program) received the highest mean ratings, while ethical behaviors and collaboration with families and community were rated lowest.

Comparing the importance ratings by gender, females rated every standard higher than did their male colleagues (Table 2.6). Independent samples t tests confirmed that significant differences were present based on gender on each standard. Females rated the importance of each of the six standards higher to their daily practice than did male respondents: shared vision of learning, $t(115) = 2.43$, $p = .020$; school culture and instructional program, $t(261) = 3.95$, $p < .001$; organizational management, $t(260) = 3.73$, $p < .001$; collaboration with families and community, $t(261) = 3.40$, $p < .001$; ethical behaviors, $t(260) = 4.63$, $p < .001$; and

Table 2.6.   Mean Importance Scores on Standards by Gender

Emphasis	n	Mean	SD	95% CI Lower	95% CI Upper
Standard 1: Shared vision of learning					
Females	73	4.32	0.64	4.17	4.46
Males	190	4.11	0.55	4.03	4.19
Standard 2: School culture and instructional program					
Females	73	4.43	0.40	4.34	4.52
Males	190	4.19	0.46	4.12	4.25
Standard 3: Organizational management:					
Females	73	4.30	0.45	4.20	4.41
Males	189	4.06	0.49	3.99	4.13
Standard 4: Collaboration with families and community					
Females	74	4.10	0.55	3.98	4.22
Males	189	3.82	0.63	3.73	3.91
Standard 5: Ethical behavior					
Females	74	4.19	0.60	4.06	4.33
Males	188	3.80	0.63	3.71	3.89
Standard 6: Political, social, economic, legal, cultural context					
Females	74	4.19	0.52	4.07	4.31
Males	189	3.96	0.60	3.87	4.04

Table 2.7.   Independent Samples *t* Test Results: Mean Importance Scores on Standards by Gender

Emphasis	t	df	p	95% CI Lower	95% CI Upper
Standard 1: Shared vision of learning	2.43	115	0.020	0.04	0.38
Standard 2: School culture and instructional program	3.95	261	< .001	0.12	0.36
Standard 3: Organizational management	3.73	260	< .001	0.12	0.38
Standard 4: Collaboration with families and community	3.40	261	< .001	0.12	0.45
Standard 5: Ethical behaviors	4.63	260	< .001	0.23	0.56
Standard 6: Political, social, economic, legal, cultural	2.89	261	< .001	0.07	0.39

political, social, economic, legal and cultural context, $t(261) = 2.89, p < .001$.

Significant differences also were found, based upon institution type, for shared vision of learning, $F(2,258) = 3.66, p = .027$, with post hoc comparisons indicating that individuals earning their endorsements from research institutions rated the importance of this standard significantly higher importance than did those from comprehensive institutions. Spearman's rho analysis was conducted for highest degree earned. Shared vision of learning was positively but weakly associated with degree attainment ($r = .15, p = .013$), with higher educational degree attainment associated with higher importance.

Programs' Emphasis of Standards
Based Upon NCLB Implementation Date

Also examined was the emphasis that superintendent preparation programs placed on the six leadership standards, based upon the time period when respondents attained their endorsements, which was defined as prior to the implementation of NCLB mandates (before 2002) or post-NCLB (2002 or later). The mean emphasis scores were analyzed for those trained pre-NCLB and post-NCLB, using independent samples t tests. For all six standards, respondents receiving superintendent training post-NCLB recorded higher mean ratings than pre-NCLB respondents, indicating that they perceived their superintendent preparation programs had a more focused inclusion of curriculum content related to the six standards in the time since NCLB mandates were implemented (Table 2.8). Significant differences were found for five standards: shared vision of learning, $t(255) = -3.33, p = .001$; school culture and instructional program, $t(255) = -2.23, p = .027$; collaboration with families and community, $t(254) = -2.79, p = .006$; ethical behaviors, $t(253) = -2.92, p = .004$; and political, social, economic, legal, and cultural context, $t(254) = -2.10$, $p = .037$. No significant differences were found for organizational management, $t(253) = -1.44, p = 0.151$.

Comparison of Standards' Emphasis in Training to
Importance in Performance

The respondents' mean ratings of the emphasis of the six standards in their superintendent preparation programs were compared to their corresponding importance ratings, using Pearson correlation. Recall that the mean emphasis scores were lower than the mean importance scores for

**Table 2.8.   Mean Emphasis Scores
for Standards by NCLB Time of Endorsement**

Standard	n	Mean	SD	95% CI Lower	95% CI Upper
Standard 1: Shared vision of learning					
Before NCLB	143	2.87	0.89	2.73	3.02
After NCLB	114	3.22	0.77	3.08	3.36
Standard 2: School culture and instructional program					
Before NCLB	143	3.01	0.77	2.88	3.13
After NCLB	114	3.22	0.72	3.09	3.35
Standard 3: Organizational management					
Before NCLB	142	3.10	0.77	2.98	3.23
After NCLB	113	3.24	0.66	3.11	3.36
Standard 4: Collaboration with families					
Before NCLB	142	2.83	0.86	2.69	2.97
After NCLB	114	3.13	0.84	2.98	3.28
Standard 5: Ethical behavior					
Before NCLB	141	2.94	0.87	2.80	3.09
After NCLB	114	3.25	0.79	3.10	3.40
Standard 6: Political, social, economic, legal and cultural context					
Before NCLB	142	3.19	0.84	3.05	3.32
After NCLB	114	3.41	0.81	3.26	3.55

each of the 39 functions within the six standards (Table 2.3), suggesting that the respondents did not perceive that their superintendency curriculum sufficiently focused on the knowledge and skills to fully prepare them for their initial appointments as school district superintendents. All relationships were positive and statistically significant, and all higher importance ratings were associated with higher emphasis ratings (Table 2.9). The relationship between emphasis and importance ratings for shared vision of learning was positive and weak to low, $r = .16$, $p = .004$; school culture and instructional program was positive and low, $r = .23$, $p < .001$; organizational management was positive and moderate, $r = .27$, $p < .001$; collaboration with families and community was positive and moderate, $r = .35$, $p < .001$; ethical behaviors was positive and moderate, $r = .39$, $p < .001$; and political, social, economic, legal, and cultural context was positive and moderate, $r = .39$, $p < .001$.

Table 2.9.   Pearson *r* Results for Emphasis and Importance

Standard	n	r	p
Shared vision of learning	313	0.16	0.004
School culture and instructional program	296	0.23	< .001
Organizational management	284	0.27	< .001
Collaboration with families and community	277	0.35	< .001
Ethical behaviors	273	0.39	< .001
Political, social, economic, legal, cultural	269	0.39	< .001

**Table 2.10.   Paired Sample *t* Test Results
Comparing Emphasis Scores to Importance**

Standard	Mean Difference	t	df	p	95% CI Lower	95% CI Upper
Shared vision of learning	−1.11	−20.36	312	< .001	−1.21	−1.00
School culture and instructional program	−1.14	−25.25	295	< .001	−1.22	−1.05
Organizational management	−0.96	−21.49	283	< .001	−1.05	−0.87
Collaboration with families and community	−0.94	−18.03	276	< .001	−1.04	−0.84
Ethical behaviors	−0.84	−16.37	272	< .001	−0.94	−0.74
Political, social, economic, legal, cultural context	−0.75	−15.23	268	< .001	−0.85	−0.65

In order to determine if the differences in mean ratings were statistically significant, a paired samples t test was conducted for each pair of ratings. The participants rated the importance of each standard to their daily practice significantly higher than they reported that the content of these standards was emphasized in their superintendent preparation programs. Significant differences were as follows: shared vision of learning, $t(312) = -20.36$, $p < .001$; school culture and instructional program, $t(295) = -25.25$, $p < .001$; organizational management, $t(283)$, -21.49, $p < .001$; collaboration with families and community, $t(276) = -18.03$, $p < .001$; ethical behaviors, $t(272) = -16.37$, $p < .001$; and political, social, economic, legal, and cultural context, $t(268) = -15.23$, $p < .001$.

Recommended Changes to Superintendent Preparation Programs

An open-ended question asked respondents to list changes that they would recommend to Illinois superintendent preparation programs, to improve their effectiveness in preparing aspiring superintendents. Responses were obtained from 178 superintendents and subsequently were categorized into themes and analyzed by respondents' gender. The most commonly stated recommendation, provided by 56 respondents (31.5%), was for programs to provide hands-on training and real-world experiences (Table 2.4). Some respondents recommended that theory be deemphasized and replaced with more practical applications in courses, while others suggested that programs include extensive paid internships in the school district central office. One stated, "I believe superintendent preparation programs need to include more meaningful internship activities. On-the-job training is extremely beneficial in order to understand the topics covered in this survey as they relate to the daily responsibilities and expectations of a superintendent." A respondent wrote, "All programs should include sufficient practical skills building, not just focus on academic 'ivory tower' knowledge. My program included a 1-year internship that built on the classroom work and served to dramatically enhance my preparation for the position."

The second most common recommendation, reported by 37 respondents (20.8%), was the need for more comprehensive training in fiscal responsibility, finance, and budget management. One male respondent stated: "More time should be spent on finance, finance, finance. Anyone can put a budget together. Where does the revenue come from? What are the limitations on its use? How do we anticipate revenue from year to year?"

The third most-cited recommendation, stated by 25 respondents (14.0%), was a desire to have either currently practicing or former superintendents employed as instructors in the superintendency program, so that they could relate theory to problems of practice by providing examples from their personal experiences. One male respondent stated,

> I believe the single most important component of an effective superintendent preparation program is to have personnel that have been actual sitting superintendents or administrators provide the instruction.... The most ineffective courses and workshops are many times taught by instructors with little or no practical experience.

Another male suggested, "I would like to see an increased number of superintendents or former superintendents serving as professors." Other recommendations were as follows: dealing with school district and

**Table 2.11.   Recommended Revisions
to Illinois Superintendent Preparation Programs**

Suggested Change	Total	%	Males	%	Females	%
Increased hands-on training/real-world experiences	56	31.5	38	30.9	18	32.7
Expanded focus on fiscal/financial concerns	37	20.8	27	22.0	10	18.2
Have practicing educational leaders teach the courses	25	14.0	14	11.4	11	20.0
Expanded focus on political issues in school/community	16	9.0	10	8.1	6	10.9
Mentor program	16	9.0	13	10.6	3	5.5
Expanded focus on board-superintendent working relationships	15	8.4	11	8.9	4	7.3
Other response	13	7.3	10	8.1	3	5.5
Total responses	178	100.0	123	100.0	55	100.0

community politics (N = 16), developing a superintendent mentoring program (N = 16), and board/superintendent relationships (N = 15).

Male and female respondents provided consistent recommendations regarding revisions to superintendent preparation. However, females were nearly twice as likely than were males to recommend that current or former superintendents serve as instructors, and males were twice as likely to recommend that mentor programs be established for novice superintendents.

DISCUSSION AND IMPLICATIONS

This study determined that Illinois public school districts superintendents generally have positive opinions of the effectiveness of their training, yet they also assert that some changes could be implemented that could enhance the effectiveness of university-based superintendent preparation programs in providing aspiring school district leaders with essential knowledge and skills for the superintendency. Despite the finding that superintendents in this study were relatively satisfied with their preparation, scholars (Hess & Kelly, 2007; Levine, 2005; Orr & Pounder, 2006; Young & Kochan, 2004) concur that there is a need to revise the superintendent preparation curriculum to remain relevant with 21st century teaching and learning and education reform mandates. The present study expands the empirical research base on superintendent preparation, by incorporating the perspectives of individuals who are actively immersed in leading Illinois public school districts. Several findings from this research merit additional discussion and are addressed in this section.

Superintendents Generally Are Satisfied With the Quality of Their Training

In this study over three fourths (78%) respondents reported that their university-based superintendent training was effective in preparing them for their positions. These ratings by Illinois superintendents were nearly identical to those reported by superintendents (78.7%) across the nation in the 2010 AASA superintendency study that was conducted during approximately the same timeframe (Kowalski et al., 2011). This finding is interesting in light of reports that have documented an increasing complexity to the superintendency (Kowalski & Brunner, 2011), due to heightened and urgent demands for school leaders to reform their organizations and to improve student achievement and that subsequently have called the adequacy of administrator preparation programs into question (Broad Foundation and Thomas B. Fordham Institute, 2003; Levine, 2005). In fact, superintendents' ratings of the quality of their training actually have improved in the past decade, as approximately two thirds of U.S. superintendents (Glass et al., 2000) rated their programs as good in 2000. In an era of rapidly increasing demands on this position, one may assume that novice superintendents may feel unprepared for the myriad responsibilities of their jobs. Thus, it was noteworthy to discover that superintendents generally have favorable opinions about the quality of their training.

Forty-six states have adopted or adapted the ISLLC standards since they were developed in 1996, requiring their use to structure the redesign of principal and superintendent preparation programming (Baker, Orr, & Young, 2007). Illinois superintendency programs have been using these standards for over a decade, implementing them in revised programming at the approximate time that NCLB legislation was enacted. Superintendents in this study who earned their licenses post-NCLB noted that the six standards were more fully emphasized than those earning this license prior to NCLB; the differences in emphasis ratings were significant for all standards with the exception of the fifth standard (ethical behaviors). Thus, it is apparent that Illinois university-based superintendent preparation programs have restructured their curricula to incorporate the content contained in the ISLLC standards.

In 2008 approximately seven in ten leadership preparation programs in the United States were reported as being accredited by the National

Council for Accreditation of Teacher Education, which uses a version of the ISLLC standards for its accreditation approval process (Hackmann & McCarthy, 2011). Similar to the state of Illinois, university-based superintendency programs across the United States have been required to revise course content to embrace the ISLLC functions. Given that half of the nation's superintendents expect to leave this position within a few years (Kowalski et al., 2011), it is very likely that administrators trained under the ISLLC standards increasingly will be hired to fill these vacancies. Of course, it is possible that veteran superintendents also may have benefitted from additional work-based experiences over the years, such as mentoring programs and professional development, that they may have found difficult to distinguish from their recollections of their superintendency training, the professional development opportunities in which they may have participated within the state through regional educational offices and professional associations. In addition, a limitation of this study was that it reported the perceptions of superintendents related to the adequacy of their training; it is possible that others (e.g., school board members, teachers, and administrators working within the school district) may have differing viewpoints regarding the superintendent's leadership skills.

Given the fact that nearly one fourth of respondents reported that their training was either ineffective (14%) or neither effective nor ineffective (9%), critics of superintendent preparation program quality also can grasp onto these data as evidence of their concerns. Are these individuals serving as successful leaders in their school districts, and if so, to what do they attribute their effectiveness? These findings are of value given the rhetoric indicating the need for change in superintendent training and voicing concerns regarding the overall quality of university programs that prepare educational leaders (Cambron-McCabe & Cunningham, 2002). Further research is warranted to more fully discern specific features of superintendent programming that are deemed deficient for those who aspire to the superintendency.

Differing Perceptions of Males and Females

Several interesting findings were discovered related to gender of the superintendents. Particularly noteworthy was the disclosure that female respondents rated the importance of the six standards as significantly more important to their superintendent practice than did their male colleagues. This finding is consistent with earlier research suggesting that female respondents routinely attribute higher ratings of importance to issues contained in research studies than do male respondents (L'Hommedieu, Menges, & Brinko, 1988, 1990). In addition, a higher proportion of females than males recommended that practicing educational leaders should teach superintendency coursework, but fewer females suggested that mentoring programs were an important support system for novice superintendents. Because the survey instrument did not ask respondents to report their previous administrative experience, we were unable to discern whether the females who participated in this study had central office administrative experience prior to entering the superintendency. However, previous research has noted that the females comprise the majority of central office administrators (Mahitivanichcha & Rorrer, 2006). Furthermore, Kowalski et al. (2011) reported that 66.5% of female superintendents compared to 37.9% of males had served as district-level coordinators, supervisors, or directors, and 50% of females compared to 33.9% of males had served as assistant, associate, or deputy superintendents. A greater proportion of women advance to the superintendency from central office positions, whereas males are more likely to transition to their initial superintendency positions from school principals. Because females are more likely to have served in central office appointments, they have had more extensive opportunities than their male counterparts have had to engage in districtwide duties and develop leadership skills that typically are associated with the superintendency. Thus, females may be better positioned to have a more comprehensive understanding of administrative knowledge and skills that need to be addressed in superintendent preparation programming.

However, it also may be possible that females were more deliberate in reflecting on and identifying discrete superintendent responsibilities that align with these leadership standards and to find them useful in promoting the development of aspiring superintendents. Additional research is needed to determine why males and females perceive these standards differently. University faculty members in leadership preparation programs should further explore these differing perspectives of males and females, in an effort to determine whether individualized learning experiences may be appropriate for different genders as they engage in the superintendency curriculum.

Curriculum Content in Superintendent Preparation and Absence of a Focus on Learning

Eighty percent of respondents rated the 39 functions within the six leadership standards for superintendent practice as important or highly important to their practice, yet only 39% reported that these functions were emphasized or highly emphasized in their preparation programs.

Respondents noted that content related to instructional leadership duties was largely missing in most preparation programs, indicating that only 38% of the instructional leadership functions included in the school culture and instructional program standard were emphasized or highly emphasized in their training, while noting that 87% of the functions linked to instructional leadership were important or highly important to practice.

In addition, every respondent rated the importance of each function higher than he/she reported that it was emphasized in programming, supporting arguments for increased integration of this content into the superintendent preparation curriculum (Grogan & Andrews, 2002; Murphy & Vriesenga, 2004). It is clear from the literature (Hackmann & McCarthy, 2011; Levine, 2005; Murphy, 2003), as well as from the perspectives of Illinois superintendents, that clearly articulated standards could serve as the foundation for leadership preparation program redesign.

In an effort to isolate the essential superintendent responsibilities that the respondents identified as deficient in their preparation, we more closely examined the 39 functions of central office administrators that were developed within the standards. Conducting a gap analysis, we calculated the difference between the mean importance and emphasis ratings on each item (the scales on each function ranged from 1-5). The differences within each function, which are reported in Table 2.3, ranged from a low of .56 to a high of 1.44, and 19 of the 39 items recorded a difference of 1.0 or higher. The functions with the largest gaps (at least 1.25) were as follows:

- developing and implementing a district improvement plan that addresses operations and student achievement (Standard 1), 1.44;
- developing methods of evaluation, accountability systems, data collection, and analysis of data to monitor student progress (Standard 2), 1.41;
- promoting the use of technologies to support effective teaching and learning (Standard 2), 1.36;
- developing strategies for providing a safe and secure district environment, including a substance-, weapon-, and violence-free work environment (Standard 3), 1.34;
- maintaining Board support for district goals for achievement and instruction (Standard 2), 1.33;
- ensuring a system of accountability for every student's academic and social success (Standard 5), 1.32;

- developing and adopting districtwide, research-based instructional goals in collaboration with school board members and principals (Standard 1), 1.27;
- developing strategies for monitoring and evaluating the district instructional plan (Standard 1), 1.25.

Arguably, these eight functions are very closely aligned with central office administrators' responsibilities to serve as learning leaders of their districts. In addition, the standards that had the highest gaps between mean importance and emphasis ratings, Standard 1 (shared vision of learning) and Standard 2 (school culture and instructional program), also are the two standards most closely aligned with learning-leadership responsibilities. Research has confirmed the importance of superintendents to create learning-centered school systems that maintain a laser-like focus on student, professional, and organizational learning (Copland & Knapp, 2006; Knapp et al., 2003). Thus, it was disappointing to discover that the greatest gaps among the 39 functions were those responsibilities that are connected to leadership for learning activities.

Prioritizing the Superintendents' Areas of Responsibility

As was noted, when rating the 39 administrative functions of superintendents, the respondents reported several deficiencies in preparation involving serving as learning leaders. Yet, despite identifying these instructional leadership concerns, when asked to suggest revisions to superintendent training, their recommendations did not encompass content related to student learning issues. Instead, the superintendents recommended the inclusion of curriculum content that included financial and political concerns, expressing a need for a more comprehensive understanding of school finance and budgeting principles, addressing school district/community politics, and maintaining effective working relationships between the superintendent and school board. A majority of respondents to 2010 AASA superintendency study (Kowalski et al., 2010) rated their academic coursework in school finance (63.6%) and school public relations (50.2%) as *extremely important*, but fewer than half gave the same importance ratings to curriculum (42.0%) and instructional methods (31.%) courses.

Even in the current accountability climate in which student achievement issues and systemic reform mandates are front and center, leadership for student learning did not appear to be the highest priority of many superintendents in this study. The simple reality may be that, although promoting student learning is the bedrock of the school system, superintendents fear that they are more likely to be fired from their positions as a result of conflicts with their school board or community or for fiscal mismanagement than they are for concerns about an inability to evidence student achievement gains. They also may choose to delegate oversight to instructional leadership issues to other administrators, including school principals and other central office administrative staff, so that they can focus their attention on other district-level responsibilities, such as community relationships and finance, that they believe are of higher importance to their continuation in their positions. Given this disconnect, additional exploration into superintendents' perceptions of their roles as learning leaders is advised. How do effective superintendents function as learning leaders, while also attending to their managerial, fiscal, and political responsibilities?

RECOMMENDATIONS

The findings from this study suggest that, while improvements have been noted in Illinois superintendent training since the implementation of NCLB, additional reforms are desirable in order to continue to address the evolving demands of this position. Several recommendations for school districts, policymakers and professional organizations, and leadership preparation programs are presented as a result of this research.

Recommendations for School Districts

When hiring school superintendents, school board members may wish to consider applicants' quality of preparation, to ensure that candidates have adequate content knowledge and skills in areas that are considered important to the board. Despite continued calls that superintendents need to effective learning leaders, only 20.0% of current superintendents report that their boards employed them because of their ability to be an instructional leader (Kowalski et al., 2011); they were more likely to indicate that they were hired because of their personal characteristics (33.5%) or their perceived potential to be a change agent (24.9%). In this study, we found that Illinois superintendents who received their training from research universities rated the importance of a shared vision of learning higher than those receiving their degrees from doctoral and comprehensive institutions. Visionary leadership is a skill that is essential to successfully navigate the challenges of 21st century leadership. School boards could consider employing superintendents who have the capacity to develop a vision for learning within their school systems and to create and implement necessary strategies to improve student outcomes.

Recommendations for Policymakers and Professional Organizations

Respondents in this study who offered suggestions for improving leadership preparation programs recommended that mentors be provided to novice superintendents. Although leadership preparation programs can create the initial mentoring experience through internship placements with successful school superintendents, universities typically do not have sufficient institutional resources to provide mentoring support to candidates once they have attained their degrees and have been placed in their formal administrative positions. State legislators and state education department officials may wish to consider providing funding to support formalized mentoring for novice superintendents, ideally through the first 2 years as school district leaders. State superintendent associations can facilitate the development of mentoring processes, matching new superintendents with veteran superintendents. In 2007, at least 18 state affiliates of the American Association of School Administrators had created some form of mentoring or coaching programs for novice superintendents (Beem, 2007).

Research on mentoring primarily has focused on the importance of mentoring women (Mahitivanichcha & Rorrer, 2006) into the superintendency due, in part, to difficulties that females historically have experienced in gaining access to this position and negotiating through established professional networks as they strive to become integrated into their roles. In this study, although mentoring was proposed by only 9% of those respondents who recommended programmatic revisions, males were twice as likely as females to suggest mentoring programs. Perhaps, because females now lead one fourth of Illinois public school districts and are more likely to ascend to the superintendency from central office positions than are males, many females may feel more confident in transitioning into this position. In contrast, males who transition into superintendency appointments through the principalship route may perceive that they do not have sufficient experience base as they move into the superintendent's desk. Regardless of one's comfort level with becoming a new superintendent, mentoring programs should be equally accessible to any individual—female or male—who believe that having the support of a veteran mentor would be beneficial in supporting her/his socialization into this position.

An additional recommendation for state policymakers and administrator associations is to provide a multitude of opportunities for continual professional development for school district leaders. The issuance of the superintendent credential should merely be considered as evidence that the educator has attained the minimal level of knowledge and skills necessary for entry into this position. Respondents in this study voiced a need for additional training in such areas as school finance, politics, board relationships, and school/community relationships. As the expectations of the position change over time, school district leaders need access to high quality professional development so that they can continue to deepen their understanding of effective leadership practices.

Recommendations for Leadership Preparation Programs

University faculty should continually examine the quality of their programming, so that they ensure that aspiring superintendents are exposed to curricular content that addresses the challenges of leading a 21st century school system. Research confirms that effective superintendent leadership can facilitate increased student achievement (Waters & Marzano, 2006), and educational leadership faculty should incorporate topics related to effective teaching and learning practices into the curriculum. Consideration could be given to the inclusion of a leadership for learning framework as an integral component of the superintendent preparation curriculum. A number of leadership models cited in the literature address instructional leadership practices of educational administrators, and they incorporate a collaboration element that emphasizes leadership of student learning (Copland & Knapp, 2006; Knapp et al., 2003; Young & Kochan, 2004). The leadership for learning approach includes aspects of the political and managerial roles, yet it focuses on leading for student learning as core to all aspects of leadership practice. The inclusion of this framework could provide successful leadership training in the area of student learning, while at the same time offering a framework that provides fidelity in training.

Additionally, university faculty should examine their curriculum and learning experiences to ensure that the following recommendations provided by respondents are adequately addressed: (a) real-world experiences, such as internships, that allow students to apply classroom theory to problems of practice; (b) enhanced content related to fiscal, finance, and budgeting issues; (c) utilization of instructors who are currently—or were recently—successful school district superintendents; (d) additional content related school/community politics; and (e) additional attention to the development of effective board/superintendent relationship. These recommendations are also supported in empirical research as program reform focal points that warrant more attention in university-based training (Kowalski et al., 2011; Levine, 2005, Orr, 2003, Waters & Marzano, 2006).

CONCLUSION

The public school superintendent's role has changed considerably over the past 30 years and superintendent preparation programs are continually challenged to keep pace with these changes. Critics have asserted that university-based superintendent training programs are not adequately preparing aspiring superintendents for the complexities of the position (Cambron-McCabe & Cunningham, 2007; Levine, 2005). Recent changes in the nature and direction of school reform have eclipsed management-focused professional preparation programs, and it therefore is important to restructure superintendent preparation programs to address the evolving roles and responsibilities inherent in the superintendency (Björk, Kowalski, & Young, 2006).

It is apparent that leadership education has become one of the public education reform strategies of the 21st century. Spotlighting leadership education presumes that improved leadership preparation and development will yield better leadership, management, and organizational practices that, in turn, will improve teaching, student learning, and student performance (Orr, 2006). This study disclosed that while a significant majority of Illinois superintendents have a favorable impression of their university-based superintendent training, they also noted that there was a significant gap between the importance of functions relative to their administrative practice and the extent to which these functions had been emphasized in their leadership preparation programs. There continues to be a debate among educational scholars about critical components of effective leadership preparation (Knapp et al., 2003; Orr & Pounder, 2006; Young & Kochan, 2004), and the findings from this study can be of assistance in identifying elements that can be strengthened in superintendent preparation.

REFERENCES

American Association of School Administrators. (1979). *Guidelines for preparation of school administrators.* Arlington, VA: Author.
American Association of School Administrators. (1993). *Professional standards for the superintendency.* Arlington, VA: Author.

Baker, B. D., Orr, M. T., & Young, M. D. (2007). Academic drift, institutional production, and professional distribution of graduate degrees in educational leadership. *Educational Administration Quarterly, 43,* 279-318. doi:10.1177/0013161X07303320

Barnett, D. (2004). School leadership preparation programs: Are they preparing tomorrow's leaders? *Education, 9*(1), 121-125.

Beem, K. (2007). Superintendent mentoring the state way. *School Administrator, 64*(4), 10-18.

Björk, L. G., & Kowalski, T. J. (2005). *The contemporary superintendent: Preparation, practice, and development.* Thousand Oaks, CA: Corwin Press.

Björk, L. G., Kowalski, T. J., & Young, M. D. (2006, April). *National education reform reports: Implications for professional preparation and development.* Paper presented at the annual meeting of the American Educational Research Association, Chicago, IL.

Broad Foundation and Thomas B. Fordham Institute. (2003). *Better leaders for America's schools: A manifesto.* Washington, DC: Author. Retrieved from http://www.broadeducation.org/asset/1128-betterleadersforamericasschools.pdf

Brunner, C., Grogan, M., & Björk, L. (2002). Shifts in the discourse defining the superintendency: Historical and current foundations of the position. In J. Murphy (Ed.), *The educational leadership challenge: Redefining leadership for the 21st century* (pp. 211-238). Chicago, IL: National Society for the Study of Education.

Callahan, R. (1966). *The superintendent of schools: A historical analysis.* St. Louis, MO: Washington University, Graduate Institution of Education. Retrieved from ERIC database. (ED010410)

Cambron-McCabe, N., & Cunningham, L. (2002). National Commission for the Advancement of Educational Leadership: Opportunity for transformation. *Educational Administration Quarterly, 38,* 289-299. doi:10.1177/0013161X02038002010

Carnegie Foundation for the Advancement of Teaching. (n.d.). *Classification descriptions.* Retrieved from http://classifications.carnegiefoundation.org/descriptions/

Commission on School Leader Preparation in Illinois Colleges and Universities. (2006). *School leader preparation: A blueprint for change. Submitted to the Illinois Board of Higher Education by the Commission on School Leader Preparation in Illinois Colleges and Universities.* Retrieved from http://www.ibhe.org/Board/agendas/2006/August/Item6fullReport.pdf

Cooper, B. S., Fusarelli, L. D., Jackson, B. L., & Poster, J. (2002). Is "superintendency preparation" an oxymoron? Analyzing change in programs, certification, and control. *Leadership and Policy in Schools, 1,* 242-255.

Copland, M. A., & Knapp, M. S. (2006). *Leadership for learning: Reflection, planning, and action.* Alexandria, VA: Association for Supervision and Curriculum Development.

Council of Chief State School Officers. (1996). *Interstate School Leaders Licensure Consortium Standards for School Leaders.* Washington, DC: Author. Retrieved from www.ccsso.org/pdfs/isllcstd.pdf

Council of Chief State School Officers. (2008). *Educational policy standards 2008: ISLLC 2008 as adopted by the National Policy Board for Educational Administration.* Washington, DC: Author.

Cunningham, L., & Hentages, J. (1982). *The American school superintendency 1982: A full report.* Arlington, VA: The American Association of School Administrators.

Darling-Hammond, L., LaPointe, M., Meyerson, D., Orr, M. T., & Cohen, C. (2007). *Preparing school leaders for a changing world: Lessons from exemplary leadership development programs.* Stanford, CA: Stanford University, Stanford Educational Leadership Institute.

Fowler, F. J. (2009). *Survey research methods.* Newbury Park, CA: SAGE.

Fry, B., Bottoms, G., O'Neill, K., & Walker, S. (2007). *Schools need good leaders now: State progress in creating a learning-centered school leadership system.* Atlanta, GA: Southern Regional Education Board. Retrieved from www.sreb.org

Glasman, N. S., & Glasman, L. D. (1997). Connecting the preparation of school leaders to the practice of school leadership. *Peabody Journal of Education, 72*(2), 3-20.

Glass, T., Björk, L., & Brunner, C. (2000). *The study of the American school superintendency, 2000: A look at the superintendent of education in the new millennium.* Arlington, VA: American Association of School Administrators.

Glass, T. E., & Franceschini, L. A. (2007). *The state of the American school superintendency: A mid-decade study.* Lanham, MD: Rowman & Littlefield Education.

Grogan, M., & Andrews, R. (2002). Defining preparation and professional development for the future. *Educational Administration Quarterly, 38,* 233-256. doi:10.1177/0013161X02382007

Hackmann, D. G., & McCarthy, M. M. (2011). *At a crossroads: The educational leadership professoriate in the 21st-century.* Charlotte, NC: Information Age.

Hess, F. M. (2003). *A license to lead? A new leadership agenda for America's schools.* Washington, DC: Progressive Policy Institute.

Hess, F. M., & Kelly, A. P. (2007). Learning to lead: What gets taught in principal-preparation programs. *Teachers College Record, 109,* 244-274.

Hoyle, J. R. (2004). *New directions for CEO superintendent leadership.* Thousand Oaks, CA: Corwin Press.

Hoyle, J. R., Björk, L. G., Collier, V., & Glass, T. (2005). *The superintendent as CEO: Standards-based performance.* Thousand Oaks, CA: Corwin Press.

Knapp, M. S., Copland, M., & Talbert, J. E. (2003). *Leading for learning: Reflective tools for school and district leaders.* Seattle, WA: University of Washington/Center for the Study of Teaching & Policy.

Kowalski, T. J. (2003). Superintendent shortage: The wrong problem and wrong solutions. *Journal of School Leadership, 13,* 288-303.

Kowalski, T. J., & Brunner, C. C. (2011). The school superintendent: Roles, challenges, and issues. In F. English (Ed.), *Handbook of educational leadership* (2nd ed.). Thousand Oaks, CA: SAGE.

Kowalski, T. J., McCord, R. S., Petersen, G. J., Young, I. P., & Ellerson, N. M. (2011). *The American school superintendent: 2010 decennial study.* Lanham, MD: Rowman & Littlefield Education.

L'Hommedieu, R., Menges, R. J., & Brinko, K. T. (1988). *The effects of student ratings feedback to college teachers: A meta-analysis and review of research.* Unpublished manuscript, Northwestern University, Center for the Teaching Professions, Evanston, IL.

L'Hommedieu, R., Menges, R. J., & Brinko, K. T. (1990). Methodological explanations for the modest effects of feedback. *Journal of Educational Psychology, 82,* 232-241.

Leithwood, K., Louis, K. S., Anderson, S., & Wahlstrom, K. (2004). *How leadership influences student learning: Review of research.* New York, NY: The Wallace Foundation.

Levine, A. (2005). *Educating school leaders.* New York, NY: The Education Schools Project.

Mahitivanichcha, K., & Rorrer, A. K. (2006). Women's choices within market constraints: Re-visioning access to the superintendency. *Educational Administration Quarterly, 42,* 483-517. doi:10.1177/0013161X06289962

Murphy, J. (2003). *Reculturing educational leadership: The ISLLC standards ten years out.* Retrieved from http://www.npbea.org/Resources/ISLLC_10_years_9-03.pdf

Murphy, J., & Vriesenga, M. (2004). *Research on preparation programs in educational administration: An analysis.* Columbia, MO: University Council for Educational Administration.

National Commission on Excellence in Education. (1983). *A nation at risk: The imperative for educational reform. A report to the Nation and the Secretary of Education, United States Department of Education.* Washington, DC: Author.

National Policy Board for Educational Administration. (1989). *Improving the preparation of school administrators.* Tempe, AZ: University Council for Education Administration.

National Policy Board for Educational Administration. (2009). *Educational leadership program standards: ELCC revised standards. First draft.* Washington, DC: Author.

Orr, M. T., & Pounder, D. (2006). *Taskforce report: Six years later and future direction.* New York, NY: Bank Street College.

Petersen, G., Fusarelli, L. D., & Kowalski, J. T. (2008). Novice superintendent perceptions of preparation adequacy and problems of practice. *Journal of Research on Leadership Education, 3*(2), 2-22.

Waters, J. T., & Marzano, R. J. (2006). *School district leadership that works: The effect of superintendent leadership on student achievement.* Denver, CO: Mid-Continent Research for Education and Learning.

Wilmore, E. L. (2008). *Superintendent leadership: Applying the Educational Leadership Constituent Council standards for improved district performance.* Thousand Oaks, CA: Corwin Press.

Young, M. D., & Kochan, F. (2004). UCEA leaders respond: Supporting leadership for America's schools. In T. J. Lasley (Ed.), *Better leaders for America's schools: Perspectives on the manifesto* (pp. 115-129). Columbia, MO: University Council for Educational Administration.

CHAPTER 3

PRINCIPAL
SUCCESSION PLANNING

How One School District Successfully
Improves the Quality and Quantity
of Principal Candidates

Shawn Joseph and Virginia Roach

ABSTRACT

American school systems face the daunting challenge of recruiting and preparing quality candidates for the demands of the secondary principalship. In a time when qualified principal candidates are difficult to find, school districts are beginning to develop district lemvel "grow your own" principal preparation programs. The purpose of this study was to conduct a comprehensive evaluation of one school district's secondary "grow your own" principal preparation program. Quantitative and qualitative methods were employed to collect and analyze data for this study. Daniel Stufflebeam's context, input, process, product model of evaluation was used to formulate 6 research questions to guide the research. The findings indicated that the secondary leadership development program increased the quantity of principal candidates within the school district, was cost effective, and participants of the program perceived themselves to have moderately high levels

Research in Learning and Teaching in Educational Leadership
pp. 55–84

of leadership behaviors. The program did help participants understand the administrative culture of the school system. Inconsistencies were found with the implementation of the program's components which required a more collaborative, systematic approach to address. The scope of the program, access to executive staff members, cohort groups of study, and the developmental team meeting were identified as strengths of the program. The content of monthly seminars, communication between the program and stakeholders, and the professional development team meetings were identified as areas of the program that needed to be improved.

THE CHALLENGE: FINDING HIGH QUALITY PRINCIPALS TO LEAD SCHOOLS

Developing school principals who are prepared with the skills, attitudes, and understanding to improve academic outcomes for all children has been a challenging endeavor in American public schools. The principalship is a job with tremendous responsibility, a high degree of complexity, and one that fewer and fewer qualified people are eager to pursue. In an era of increased accountability and expectations for schools, it is important to have an excellent principal in every school (Edmonds, 1979; Murphy, 2002; Waters, Marzano, & McNulty, 2003). Good principals set expectations, monitor curriculum implementation, supervise teachers, monitor student performance, and set the tone for the climate of a school (Witziers, Bosker, & Kruger, 2003). Researchers have reported a direct correlation between principal leadership and school-based achievement levels (Leithwood, Louis, Anderson, & Wahlstrom, 2004; Waters et al., 2003).

Given the importance of the principal and the complexity of the job, a principal shortage is a national concern. According to the Educational Research Services (2000), there are fewer and fewer candidates prepared to assume the role and responsibilities of the principalship in American schools. The job has not been viewed as a desirable position by educators due to the stress, complexity, accountability, and compensation for the position (Copeland, 2001; Hallinger, 1992; Murphy, 1994; Murphy & Hallinger, 1992; Portin, 1997; Portin, Shen & Williams, 1998; Tirozzi, 2001; Whitaker, 2003). The principal shortage is not just an issue of quantity; there have also been concerns regarding the quality of principal candidates graduating from preparation programs (Murphy & Forsyth, 1999).

Schools of education and their educational leadership preparation programs have been criticized for their recruitment practices, instructional leadership preparation, professional development, licensure standards, and little use of real-world problems and experiences (National

Commission on Excellence in Educational Administration, 1987; Murphy, 1990; Milstein & Krueger, 1997). Other reports emphasized revising core curricula to focus on rigor, instructional practice and ethics, raising standards for licensure and certification, and stressing relevance and clinical experience (Levine, 2005; Murphy, 1990). Still others have called for traditional principal preparation programs to be abolished and replaced with alternative programs that were created and implemented by schools, districts, and states instead of universities (The Broad and Fordham Foundations, 2003). If graduate schools of education are not adequately preparing candidates to assume principalships, and if the shortage in the pipeline to the principalship continues, districts will face dire shortages in applicants for this critical position. In response, school districts have devised creative ways to maintain the quantity and quality of principal candidates for their schools (Wallace Foundation, 2012).

In an attempt to address the national concern regarding the supply of well-qualified principal candidates, school districts across the nation have attempted to increase the quantity and quality of principal candidates within their school districts through developing grow your own principal preparation programs (Dodson, 2006; Morrison, 2005). Some of these programs have been in partnership with local universities, whereas others have been solely developed and implemented by their school districts (Baitland, 1992; Cox, 1998; Mercado, 2002; Newman, 2004).

One such school district was the Northwest School District,[1] located in the mid-Atlantic region of the United States. The Northwest School District was the largest school district within its state during the study. The Northwest School District had both suburban and urban characteristics, and it was one of the most demographically diverse school districts in the state. The racial make-up of the school district during the time of this study was the following: 22.9% African American, .03% American Indian, 15.2% Asian, 21.5% Hispanic, and 40.1% White. One fourth of the students within the district qualified for free or reduced-price meals. Known as a high-performing district, the average SAT score across all subtests for the district during the time of the study was 1624 out of 2400.

PROMISING PRACTICE: DEVELOPING A "GROW YOUR OWN" DISTRICT-RUN PRINCIPAL TRAINING PROGRAM

The Northwest "grow your own program" was developed as part of the districtwide Professional Growth System (PGS). The system was designed to direct how aspiring administrators would be selected, trained, evaluated, and retained over time based upon six standards derived from the nationally utilized Interstate School Leaders Licensure Consortium standards. While discussion was started in the district in 1997, the program got a major push in 1999 when a new superintendent was hired in Northwest. That superintendent dramatically increased the investment in the principal development program at both the elementary and secondary level by creating the position of director of elementary and secondary leadership development.

Under the direction of the director on elementary and secondary leadership development, the district devised a more comprehensive development and induction program for aspiring principals. Monthly cohorts were established around the principals' evaluation instrument. Principals met monthly for 2 years in cohorts and in five development meetings with their principal mentor, an outside consultant, and a district executive to engage in their own professional development as aspiring principals. After their first two initial years, the elementary principals implemented a year-long internship in their schools for aspiring educational leaders. This was an additional position given to the elementary schools.

The Northwest School District began implementation of the Administrative and Supervisory Professional Growth System (A&S PGS) in the 2003-2004 school year with 50 principals who were evaluated under the new system. During the 2004-2005 school year, the implementation was expanded to all 200 principals, school based administrators, and central office administrators. A 6-week secondary internship was added for secondary administrators. The elementary internship was reduced to 6 weeks due to budgetary restraints. In addition, the elementary internship was used to fill assistant principal vacancies instead of being an additional position.

The A&S PGS in the Northwest School District recognized that administrative leadership is "complex, changing, and essential to improving teaching and learning" (Northwest School District A&S PGS Handbook 2006-2007, p. 3). It describes the purpose of the district's professional growth system for administrators as the following:

- provides a comprehensive system for developing and evaluating administrators and supervisors;
- sets clear expectations about the roles and responsibilities for each administrative and supervisory position;
- describes professional growth opportunities to support and nurture all administrators and supervisors;
- creates a dynamic structure for critical reflection, continuous improvement, and lifelong learning; and
- promotes personal ownership of professional development and incorporates self and peer appraisal (p. 3).

With the creation of the professional growth system for administrators, the school system developed six administrative standards for principals and other school based administrators including assistant principals. The steering committee that developed these standards drew largely from the ISLLC standards to create their own six standards for the school district (Northwest School District A&S PGS Handbook 2006-2007). The standards undergirding the A&S PGS are the following:

Standard I: Each assistant principal, assistant student administrator, and coordinator of a school-based program is an educational leader who promotes success for all students as he/she facilitates the development, articulation, implementation, and stewardship of a vision of teaching and learning that is shared and supported by the school community.

Standard II: Each assistant principal, assistant student administrator, and coordinator of a school-based program is an educational leader who promotes success for all students as he/she nurtures and sustains a school culture of professional growth, high expectations, and an instructional program conducive to student learning and staff professional growth.

Standard III: Each assistant principal, assistant student administrator, and coordinator of a school-based program is an educational leader who promotes success for all students as he/she ensures the management of the organization, operations, and resources for a safe, efficient, and effective learning environment.

Standard IV: Each assistant principal, assistant student administrator, and coordinator of a school-based program is an educational leader who promotes success for all students as he or she collaborates with the school staff and other stakeholder groups including students, families, and community members.

Standard V: Each assistant principal, assistant student administrator, and coordinator of a school-based program is an educational leader who promotes success for all students as he/she models professionalism and professional growth in a culture of continuous improvement.

Standard VI: Each assistant principal, assistant student administrator, and coordinator of a school-based program is an educational leader who promotes success for all students as he/she understands, responds to, and influences the larger political, social, socioeconomic, legal, and cultural context.

THE NORTHWEST SCHOOL DISTRICT
LEADERSHIP DEVELOPMENT PROGRAM

The Northwest School District developed a principal training program at the secondary (middle and high school) and elementary levels to address its district's needs to increase the quality and quantity of principal candidates. The program began in the 1990s and has evolved over time.

This study focused on the secondary leadership development program. There are three distinct programs under the umbrella of the secondary leadership development program: the Assistant Student Administrator (ASA) program, the Secondary Assistant Principal 1 (AP1) and Assistant Principal 2 (AP2) program, and the Aspiring Principal Program (AP3). The ASA program is for entry-level middle school and high school administrative candidates. Administrative candidates in the ASA program may or may not possess an initial administrative certification. Participants in this program function as 11-month administrators and serve on a secondary school's administrative team. ASAs are not allowed to write evaluations, but they can conduct and write teacher observations. ASAs participate in monthly training meetings with their cohort group facilitated by the director of secondary leadership development. The second program, the Secondary AP1 and AP2 program, is for middle and high school administrative candidates. All participants in the Secondary AP1 and AP2 program must be certified by the state as qualified for an entry-level administrative position. Administrative candidates participate in a 2-year program including monthly seminars as a cohort. They also participate in a professional development team meeting with their principal, an outside principal consultant, and a central office supervisor. The third program, AP3, is for experienced assistant principals, and it assists these administrators with preparing for the principal interview process within the school district. The program also includes a 4-week internship where the administrative candidates assume the responsibilities of the principalship. High performing administrative candidates are selected from the total pool of assistant principals within the school district to participate in this program. While highly selective, the AP3 program diminished over time due to budgetary constraints. Participation in the AP3 program is not a requirement for obtaining a principalship within the school district.

The secondary leadership development program was designed to assist participants in developing the knowledge, skills, strategies, attitudes, and aspirations to become effective school-based leaders and to improve student learning. The program was developed to be a multiyear program for new administrators to assist candidates in demonstrating the knowledge, skills, and dispositions described in the school district's standards for administrators. Components of the Northwest Leadership Development Program were described as follows:

1.   Long-term and planned: At the secondary level, new administrators begin as an assistant student administrator or an assistant principal 1 (AP1) and progress to an assistant principal 2 (AP2).

Selected candidates can move to an assistant principal 3 (AP3 or aspiring principal) year to be trained to move into a principalship.

2. Focused on student achievement: Each participant develops a professional development plan that is based upon evidence of student learning. In addition, there are trainings which include content to help participants develop an understanding of teaching, learning, and school improvement.

3. Job-embedded: All participants of the program are placed in a full-time administrative position and the principal where they are placed is the primary trainer. The participant's professional development plan is aligned with their assigned school's improvement goals.

4. Customized, but aligned with district goals: Training for each participant balances meeting the individual needs of the participant and the needs of the organization.

5. Supportive of reflective practice: The trainings are designed to develop reflective practitioners who can plan, act, and reflect. AP1 and AP2 participants have a development team that consists of the assistant principal or intern, the school principal, a community superintendent or director of school performance, and a principal training representative or principal outside consultant. Each participant completes a portfolio that will be shared at a development team meeting. There are five development team meetings scheduled throughout the school year. Development team members are encouraged to challenge and push interns to think and grow.

6. Provides opportunities to work, discuss, and problem solve with peers: Participants are required to attend monthly seminars with a cohort of peers. Cohort groups participate in skill building, analyze case studies and critical incidents, and exchange ideas and consult about problems. There is a week-long summer training component and a 2-day residential component.

Prior to the AP1 year, candidates submit a resume, three references, participate in a Gallup phone interview, and submit a writing sample. Candidates must have at least 3 years of teaching prior to applying. Once a candidate is selected, he or she completes a self-assessment and develops a professional development plan in conjunction with his or her principal. The AP1 participates in quarterly development team meetings and monthly professional development seminars. The monthly seminars are in a cohort format with other AP1s, and the trainings are developed by the secondary director of leadership development. After the second development team meeting, the AP1 has a midyear evaluation. At this time, the AP1 can revise his or her professional development plan, set new goals, or revise development needs. After the fourth development meeting, the AP1 receives a final evaluation. The final evaluation includes input from the development team and is based upon the school district principal standards. A determination is made at the end of the year to promote the AP1 into his or her AP2 year, have the AP1 repeat his or her AP1 year, or to exit the program in consultation with human resources.

A candidate advances to his or her AP2 year in the same school as assigned in the AP1 year. A professional development plan is created based upon attainment of AP1 outcomes. The AP2 has 5 development team meetings with one of the meetings being a midyear evaluation. Similar to the AP1 year, the AP2 attends monthly seminars with his or her cohort of AP2s. At the midyear evaluation, an AP2 can revise his or her professional development plan or reevaluate development needs based upon performance. At the end of the AP2 year, the AP2 is named an assistant principal by the Northwest District Board of Education. If an AP2 has not met the standards of the program, he or she can repeat the AP2 year or work with human resources and the community superintendent to determine the best placement for the candidate. An AP2 can be recommended to enter the AP3 program by his or her community superintendent. The benefit of being an AP 3 is the exposure candidates get from executive staff and the opportunity to complete an internship experience.

Thus, the Northwest School District created a multitiered system to develop principal candidates from within the ranks of existing district employees. The system allows for extended preparation and, should a candidate not be successful, continued employment in the system. In this way the process was designed to be developmental, not punitive.

By developing their own principal preparation programs, school districts are hoping to increase both the quantity and quality of principals; however, empirical investigations are limited on school district grow your own principal training programs (Miracle, 2006; Morrison, 2005). The program at Northwest District had not been evaluated due to budgetary constraints and the belief that it was working well due to the increased number of eligible people in the administrative pool, the increasing test scores within the district, and the number of home grown principals that were successful in their jobs. This evaluation study was undertaken in 2008, four years after the first full cohort began the program.

RESEARCH QUESTIONS FOR THE STUDY

The purpose of this study was to examine one school system's effort to create and implement a "grow your own" principal preparation program. Given the paucity of "grow your own" program evaluations, such a study can be useful to other districts thinking about developing grow your own programs. This study was guided by the following research questions:

1. What factors led school authorities to the decision to develop the secondary principal preparation program?
2. What resources (financial, facilities, human) were made available in the initial design of the secondary principal preparation program?
2a. What resources (financial, facilities, human) were made available over time to implement the secondary principal preparation program?
3. To what extent do the structures of the secondary principal preparation program reflect current research about effective principal preparation programs?
4. Is the program being implemented as designed?
5. Is the secondary leadership development program perceived to be an effective aspiring principal training program?
6. What areas of the secondary principal preparation program did participants see as strengths or as needing improvement?

Conceptual Framework for Study

This study utilized the CIPP (context, input, process, product) evaluation model (Stufflebeam, 2000). The purpose of the CIPP model was to illustrate how evaluation could contribute to the decision-making process in program management (Gall, Borg, & Gall, 1996). The CIPP evaluation model answers the following questions: (a) Context: What needs to be done? (b) Input: How should it be done? (c) Process: Are things being done? and (d) Product: What are the results?

Context

Context evaluations assess needs, problems, assets, and opportunities within a specific educational setting (Gall et al., 1996). According to Stufflebeam (2000), context evaluations "are useful for judging already established goals and for helping the audience assess the effort's significance in meeting beneficiaries' needs" (p. 287). Data collection methodologies that are often used with context evaluations include reviewing documents, interviewing beneficiaries and stakeholders, conducting surveys, and analyzing demographic or performance data. Background information on the target population is also examined. Based on a review of the literature, this context evaluation included the following areas:

1. Role of the principal;
    (a) Perceived forces that led to the need for a school district to develop a training program;
    (b) Demographic data of principals during the time of program development;
    (c) Attrition rates of principals during the time of development;
2. Principal shortages experienced by the district;
    (a) Perceived root causes of shortage during the time of program development;
3. Perceived shortcomings of traditional preparation programs at the time of program development;
4. "Grow Your Own Programs";
    (a) Perceived benefit of developing a district-level training program at the time of program development.

In summary, the context evaluation was designed to answer the questions: Why was the secondary principal training program developed and what were the goals that were established for the program?

Input

Input evaluation identifies the resources and strategies needed to accomplish program goals and objectives (Gall et al., 1996). According to Stufflebeam (2000), input evaluation assesses one's existing practice and whether or not the existing practice is appropriate compared to what is being done elsewhere or is proposed in educational research literature. The educational research literature on resources related to the development of aspiring principal programs identified the following as resource considerations: principal candidate professional development, the internship experience, the cost to evaluate the program, and mentoring from experienced administrators (Bottoms, O'Neill, Frye, & Jacobson, 2004; Browne-Ferrigno, 2001; Educational Research Services, 2000; Jackson & Kelley, 2002; Maryland Task Force on the Principalship, 2000).

In summary, the input evaluation intended to answer questions such as: How is the secondary principal training program funded? Were there barriers to implementing effective research-based practices due to funding limitations?

Process

Process evaluation is evaluation of the program's implementation, after the design phase, when it is in operation (Gall et al., 1996). Stufflebeam (2000) wrote, "Process evaluation is an ongoing check on a plan's implementation plus documentation of the process, including changes in the plan as well as key omissions and/or poor execution of certain procedures" (p. 294). In short, the process evaluation should report how observers and participants judge the quality of the process.

In this study, the process evaluation included data to understand the systems that were put in place to monitor implementation of the program. The evaluation also included information detailing who was involved in the program and how program goals were communicated and enforced with all members of the program. A process check between what the educational literature identifies as best practices and the actual elements of the program of study was also conducted.

Product

Product evaluation relates to the extent to which program goals have been achieved (Gall et al., 1996). Stufflebeam (2000) asserted that product evaluation should measure, interpret, and judge an enterprise's achievement, including intended and unintended outcomes, positive and negative outcomes, as well as long-term outcomes.

In this study, the product evaluation answered the following questions: What is the perception of the effectiveness of the program by key stakeholders? To what extent did participants gain critical skills needed to successfully assume a principalship? Did participation in the program increase the pool of applicants for the principalship and increase motivation for potential principal candidates?

METHODOLOGY AND STUDY DESIGN

Quantitative and qualitative methods were employed to collect and analyze data for this study. Stufflebeam's CIPP model of evaluation was used to formulate six research questions to guide the research. Data were collected to address each component of this model—context, input, process, and product. Personal interviews were conducted with the school district's executive staff, former executive staff, the director of secondary leadership development, the administrative union president, and administrative interns (AP3s). Focus group interviews were conducted with principals, principal consultants, and 2nd-year participants of the program (AP 2s). Documents were also analyzed. The Leadership Practices Inventory-Self (LPI-Self) was also administered to 88 former participants of the program with a response rate of 67%. An ANCOVA was used to analyze the quantitative data in this study.

Matrixes were developed to triangulate qualitative data and to identify emerging themes. The ANCOVA was used to determine whether participants of the AP 3 program had higher perceptions of their leadership than participants who had not participated in the AP 3 program.

FINDINGS

Context Evaluation

A number of factors led the Northwest School District to develop a secondary principal development program. The most significant factor was the lack of qualified candidates interested in administrative positions within the school district. Similar to national trends, the district had a number of principal candidates that were eligible to retire, but it did not have a large pool of potential principal applicants. This concern resulted in the district researching ways to increase the pool of applicants so it would be able to recruit and train a principal workforce.

Faced with dwindling interest in administrative positions within the district, there was also a concern regarding the ability of principal candidates to handle the complexity of the principalship within the school district. The Northwest School District is a large, complex school district and is considered a high-performing district. There was a perception that additional training beyond the university preparation programs was needed to help principals be successful in this school district. The demands and high expectations of parents, high accountability standards from within the district and state, the political environment of the school district, and the ambitious goals of the board of education all contributed to the complexity of the principalship in the Northwest School District.

Executive staff members also expressed a desire to inculcate potential principal candidates with the culture of the school system. The superintendent and deputy superintendent of schools spoke of a specific "brand" that is associated with the school district. The school district was described as complex and political; executive staff members believed that creating a training program would be beneficial by allowing principal candidates to build relationships with different members of the school district. It would also give participants an understanding of how things were done within the school district. The deputy superintendent shared that this superintendent was very conscious of the school district's "brand". Higher achievement results brought about higher public confidence in the schools, which gave the superintendent the political clout to obtain more funding for the schools when times were good. The Northwest School District took pride in its reputation, and it believed the training program was necessary to help school administrators get results and understand of how things were done within the school district.

Finally, there was a clear commitment to build the capacity of individuals within the school system. The superintendent of schools believed the only way the school system was going to be able to effectively execute and achieve the goals of the board of education's strategic plan was for the school system to invest in developing its leaders. The Northwest School District described itself as a results-oriented school system, and executive staff believed the only way results were going to be achieved was with a high-performing workforce.

Input Evaluation

Records regarding the cost of the program at its inception were not available; however, a former executive staff member noted that the costs and resources of the program had not changed over time, with the exception of the program's cutting "training representatives" from its budget. Training representatives were consultants that worked with the principal, outside principal consultant, and the director of school performance or community superintendents on the developmental team meetings. The training representative job functions were incorporated into the duties of the principal consultants when the position was cut. Lack of financial data was a recurring theme in the process evaluation of this study: there was a need for stronger accountability measures over the implementation of the secondary leadership development program. Based upon the data that were shared, the secondary leadership development program was less expensive than other nationally job-embedded programs.

The total cost of implementing the secondary training program was $471,761. This cost does not include the time that was invested by executive staff members and offices throughout the school district to support the training of administrators. This school district effectively maximized the use of its existing offices by having the majority of offices in the school system working with the secondary leadership training program—presenting system policies, procedures, and best practices to administrative candidates. A total of 105 individuals participated in the secondary training program during the 2008-2009 school year. The average cost per participant was $4,493. When compared to the cost of training a participant in a nationally developed nonprofit principal development program, the cost of the school district's program was substantially cheaper.

The executive staff member responsible for the operating budget felt that the system was able to run this program effectively without it being too expensive. He shared that comparable trainings at a university for the amount of training participants received would be much more costly. One of the major financial limitations that he and other stakeholders identified to the overall implementation of the program was implementing an internship at the secondary level. The internship is limited to 1 month in length and the number of internships was limited to five per year since its inception due to the cost of the program. Completing the internship is not a requirement to obtaining a principalship within the school district, but the limited amount of openings for participants limits the potential benefit to having the internship. System leaders and participants all recognized the need to increase the number of internships and the length of time of each internship, but they were not able to do so because of the costs and because there was opposition by some secondary principals due to their limited knowledge of the program.

Process Evaluation

The entrance standards for the administrative pool, to a limited extent, align with the realities and duties of the principalship. The chief entrance standards are: 3 years of teaching experience, three letters of recommendation, and a writing sample. A former executive staff member who was responsible for the district's training unit stated that one of the major improvements the program needed to make was strengthening the entrance requirements for the program. The Northwest School District standards for administrative evaluation delineate a number of areas that are aligned with the demands of the principalship including creating a shared vision, sustaining school culture, managing resources, continuous improvement, and influencing political, social, economic, legal, and cultural context. The program's present entrance requirements do not align with the standards that candidates are eventually evaluated upon. Executive staff members and program implementers expressed concern with the overall quality of the pool of applicants. All applicants were not accepted into the pool; however, it appeared that the standards could be more rigorous and selective as described in the research literature. Participants were not required to demonstrate their proficiency related to standards prior to assuming an administrative role. Interviews should also be a component of the entrance requirements. Hence, while the program itself and the evaluation system is standards based, the entrance requirements to the program are not.

Aside from the entrance requirements, another concern raised was the internship. The internship had been implemented within the school district to a limited extent. Financial and political factors had limited the number of internships and the length of the internships at the secondary level. Several executive staff members and stakeholders recognized that secondary principals were not very receptive to the idea of a secondary internship. The visibility and stature of the high school position in a politically charged school district made allowing an inexperienced aspiring principal to run a school by himself or herself for an extended time difficult to approve. At the time of this research, secondary interns assumed the role and the responsibilities of the principalship within the school district for 4 weeks at a secondary school. Program participants and executive staff members asserted that this length of time was not long enough to provide interns with an authentic principal experience. One AP3 shared that she felt that some of the people would simply wait for her 1 month to be over to have the tough decisions made by the building principal when he returned.

To a great extent, the secondary leadership development program emphasized reflective practice. The program provided opportunities for extensive reflection through the professional development team meetings, through working with outside consultants, and through the monthly seminars when all of those structures functioned as designed. Participants were required to reflect in writing and orally, and participants perceived these structured opportunities for reflection to be beneficial to their growth as administrators. Despite some of the positive responses that were given about the nature of their opportunities for reflection, AP1s, AP2s, AP3s, principals, and the administrative union president questioned the relevance of the reflective opportunities provided in the monthly seminars. Time that was not spent specifically developing administrative candidates' technical skill set was deemed as "fluff", "a waste of time", and "irrelevant" by different stakeholders.

In addition, the secondary leadership development program provided an extensive mentorship program through experienced administrators. Participants were provided with a number of opportunities to be mentored by veteran administrators. Outside principal consultants were assigned to all participants in the program. In addition, a community superintendent or a director of school performance met with participants on five different occasions during the course of the school year to support participants' growth. Participants also were introduced to a number of administrators from different offices through participation in monthly seminars. In addition, participants received support from the director of secondary leadership development.

Relationships were fostered by design as participants in the secondary leadership development program participated in cohort groups. Over the course of the 2 or 3 years participants were in the program, they met monthly and trained together. Participants were given opportunities to share best practices and offer suggestions to one another. They viewed their ability to come together to learn and share as a strength of the program. Many participants that ascended to principalships commented on how the relationships that were fostered through their experiences as a cohort member in the secondary leadership development program continued to be beneficial to them in their roles as principals. All stakeholders described the lasting, trusting relationships that were developed through the use of cohort learning models.

The Northwest School District secondary leadership development program was not consistently being implemented as designed. There were concerns expressed about the development of the content of the monthly seminars. The program received an annual review, but principals, administrative participants, and the union president did not believe participants were consistently being trained on relevant topics. The director of secondary leadership development felt that the annual review of the program and the program's content was adequate, but stakeholders, including principals, the administrative union president, AP1s, AP2s, and AP3s did not feel that there was enough input and communication regarding the content of the monthly seminars. The need for collaboration in the development of seminars was identified as a concern for the program and its implementation.

Participants cited a concern regarding the principals' ability to serve as primary trainers. Although the principal accounted for 88% of the training of an administrative participant, there was limited training provided to the principals themselves. As a result, training and experiences varied among the administrative participants, based upon their work location and the experiences of the supervising principal. Further, stakeholders, including the administrative union president and the executive staff member responsible for the office that evaluates schools and principals, reported that some principals did not want to serve as principal trainers but were required to do so simply because they had an administrative vacancy in their schools. The executive staff member responsible for the office that oversees schools and principals shared that the Northwest School District is beginning to rethink how administrative candidates are assigned to trainers and his office was interested in ensuring that his best principal trainers work with administrative candidates. Yet, at the time of this study, vacancies dictated who the principal trainer was for administrative candidates.

Participants and stakeholders saw the value in having principal consultants, but they reported inconsistency in how the job was performed. Some principal consultants communicated effectively with participants and principals and some did not. There was also inconsistency regarding the amount of time principal consultants provided program participants. Although principal consultants were supposed to work 5 hours per month with AP2s and 8 hours per month with AP1s, stakeholders reported inconsistency with some outside consultants giving more hours than was required while other outside consultants worked less that the required amount of hours.

Another weak area of implementation was the professional development team meetings. There was inconsistency regarding acceptable standards of performance for administrative participants across the professional development team meetings. The administrative union president, principals, and outside principal consultants reported instances in which underperforming candidates' were allowed to exit the program with a rating of proficient. Performance outcomes of the program were evaluated subjectively, thereby causing a variance in expectations and performance between different development teams.

Product Evaluation

The Northwest School District's secondary leadership development program was created to attract and retain more qualified applicants for the principalship, to support administrative candidates in dealing with the complexities of the principalship within the district, to inculcate school district culture to administrative candidates, and to build the capacity of administrative participants so the district would have a cadre of qualified applicants to assume principal vacancies. Overall, the secondary leadership development program was perceived to be an effective secondary principal development program. The superintendent, deputy superintendent of schools, and the chief performance officer all commented on the fact that the districts secondary schools are performing at high levels, even with increased challenges of poverty, limited English proficiency, and mobility. The high performance of schools within the school district and the number of successful principals who were trained within the program led stakeholders to this view. Participants developed a firsthand knowledge of the school district and school district culture through multiple perspectives of school district presenters and speakers at monthly seminars and at their professional development team meetings. Participants were also given support at professional development team meetings by gaining insight to problems from experienced administrators. Participants had numerous interactions with school district leaders and program implementers. The secondary development leadership program did increase the number of potential principal candidates within the school system. The quality of principal candidates was considered strong, but findings were not conclusive that the strength of candidates was a result of training received through the principal training program or their previous experiences prior to entering the training program.

Most AP2s and AP3s perceived themselves as having a moderately high level of leadership based upon an analysis of their mean score on the Leadership Practices Inventory-Self Evaluation (LPI-Self). This finding suggested that participants, after completing the core program, perceived themselves to have moderately strong leadership abilities.

The results from the one-way analysis of covariance (ANCOVA), with a covariate of administrative experience, revealed a statistically nonsignificant difference ($p < .05$) in perceived leadership behaviors between the AP2s and the AP3s. Both groups perceived themselves as having moderately high levels of leadership.

Program Strengths as Reported by Various Stakeholders

The scope of the program was deemed a strength of the secondary leadership development training program. Overall, stakeholders believed the complexity of the program and the vision of supporting administrative candidates to be beneficial to administrative participants. Participants learned through hands-on experiences as they worked in administrative positions, they learned in seminar formats at the monthly meetings, and they had opportunities to critically reflect during the professional development team meetings.

The professional development team meeting process was also viewed as a strength of the program. Giving participants an opportunity to interact with executive staff and to critically reflect upon their practices was considered beneficial to administrative program participants when the team was functioning well. The deputy superintendent of schools and the executive staff member for human resources both described this process as an intimate opportunity for the executive staff to get to know candidates and provide them with critical reflection opportunities that would contribute to the candidates' development.

In a large, complex school system, having access to executive staff was identified as a strength of the secondary principal development program. Executive staff members, through the program, were given the opportunity to interact with potential administrative candidates. The administrative candidates also received an opportunity to gain systemwide insight from administrative staff and benefited from reflecting with veteran systemwide leaders.

The component of the program that is universally viewed positively is the cohort groups of study. All stakeholders commented on the benefit of having candidates foster positive relationships through learning together. Participants, principals, and executive staff agree that in a large, complex school system, having a system of support was beneficial to administrative program participants. Participants reported developing high levels of trust with one another as a result of the cohort groups; they also indicated that the cohort groups also assisted with improving reflection opportunities.

Areas of Improvement as Reported by Stakeholders

One area of improvement identified is the content of the monthly seminars. Stakeholders considered some of the content of the monthly seminars not relevant to administrative candidates. Stakeholders also want a more collaborative approach to developing the content of the monthly seminars. Specifically, stakeholders thought the monthly seminars need to be more concrete to assist administrative candidates in performing their day-to-day responsibilities; they also mentioned the need for less emphasis on exposing candidates to educational theory.

While the professional development teams were viewed as a strength, they were equally viewed as an area that needs to be improved. Concern was noted regarding the inconsistency of teams in ensuring administrative candidates demonstrated proficiency on administrative standards prior to successfully completing the program. There was also concern about team members (principals, outside consultants, mentors, and central office supervisors) being sufficiently trained to perform their duties effectively.

Communication between the leadership of the secondary leadership development program and its stakeholders was identified as an area of needed improvement. Participants, principals, and executive administrators thought a more collaborative approach should be taken to gather feedback regarding training topics for administrative candidates. There was also interest in gaining more information regarding training opportunities for stakeholders to better assist administrative candidates. Other stakeholders thought more communication regarding the structure and implementation of aspects of the program was needed in order for all stakeholders to execute their duties effectively.

Summary of Findings

The Northwest School District created a secondary leadership development program because it was concerned with the lack of qualified candidates pursing the principalship; it wanted to support administrators' capacity to handle the complexity of the job; it wanted to create and pre-serve a school culture; and it wanted to build the capacity of the organiza-tion. The secondary leadership development program increased the number of principal candidates within the school district, and partici-pants of the program perceived themselves to have moderately high lev-els of leadership behaviors. The school system presently cannot determine whether the program has increased the quality of administra-tive candidates, but the program is perceived positively due to the overall strength of principals who have been trained in the program who are cur-rently leading secondary schools within the school district. The secondary leadership development program appeared to be cost effective based upon the variety of outcomes of the program. Yet, inconsistencies were found with the implementation of the program's components. Strengths of the program included the scope of the program, access to executive staff members, cohort groups of study, and the developmental team meet-ings. The content of monthly seminars, communication between the pro-gram and stakeholders, and the professional development team meetings were identified as areas of the program that needed to be improved.

DISCUSSION OF FINDINGS

A number of this study's findings were supported by previous research conducted on grow your own principal development programs. Similar to previous research (Miracle, 2006; Morrison, 2005), this study found the school district perceived a need to continue to implement the grow your own principal training programs. As with other grow your own programs, the Northwest School District program has increased the numbers of applicants that are able to assume principalships within school district, and the programs have provided administrative participants with sup-port, exposure, and knowledge to perform the duties of a school based administrator within their district. Yet, the extent of the knowledge partic-ipants gain through the program is unknown.

Morrison (2005) and Miracle (2006) found that grow your own princi-pal training programs may not be receiving the critical analysis they need to improve, also a finding in this study. The Northwest School District was investing a substantial amount of money into the implementation of a secondary leadership development program; however, there was a lack of critical, continuous evaluation of the program. There were few account-ability measures in place to assist program developers with improving the program, and there was a lack of objective measures to determine whether or not the program was improving administrative participants' skills.

Miracle (2006) found inconsistency among principals in preparing the assistant principals in the school district in his study, a finding in the present study, as well. An administrative training program is significantly limited if the primary trainer does not take his or her role seriously or if the primary trainer is ill equipped to train administrative candidates. One challenge the Northwest School District faced was ensuring that each administrative candidate was trained by a principal that was willing and able to conduct effective training. Principals within the district became principal trainers by default due to administrative vacancies within their buildings. Furthermore, some of these principal trainers were relatively inexperienced themselves, limiting their ability to help others. While this was often expressed as frustration and a lack of communication, this could be, in fact, a call for support.

Morrison (2005) found that grow your own programs need systemwide leadership to be effective, and that was a finding in the present study. One major issue found with the secondary leadership development program was that system leaders were not clear about the philosophy of the program. Was the program designed to develop the technical skills of administrative candidates or was the program designed to develop the reflective nature of future administrators to deal with adaptive challenges that would be presented to them as school based administrators? Was the program designed to accomplish both tasks? Was this truly a principal development program or was it an assistant principal development program? It was not clear whether there was greater emphasis on acculturating and socializing administrators into their new roles as a form of an induction program or whether the intent was to systematically develop the quality and skill set of candidates. Different system leaders had different philosophies on the nature of the program, and as a result, clear expectations were not communicated or established. A clear vision for the leadership program was not established which has resulted in a negative tension among stakeholders.

This study also generated findings not found in previous research. In this study, no statistical difference was found in the perceived leadership behaviors of AP2s and the perceived leadership behaviors of AP3s. One possible reason for this result is that the sample size for the statistical analysis conducted was not large enough to render a statistical difference. Another possible reason is that all of the candidates surveyed had at least 2 full years of experience as an administrator and at least 5 years' experience in education. Because none of the participants were new to education or new to administration, they may have perceived their leadership behaviors at higher levels than what was actually demonstrated. Another potential reason that a statistically significant difference was not rendered among the two different groups of program participants could lie in the fact that the AP3 program did not formally train participants based upon standards as did the AP1 program and the AP2 program. The AP3 program prepared candidates for interviews and assisted principal candidates in understanding the political context of the school district. As has been previously mentioned, the Northwest School District is a complex, political school district. To strengthen the likelihood of internal candidates winning interviews for principalships, the district prepared AP3s for the interview situation as a focus as opposed to continuing to support candidates' leadership development. As a result, the perceived leadership behaviors could have been viewed as comparable.

One significant finding in this study is that the cost of implementing a secondary principal development training program in a school district can be manageable if the school district is training large numbers of administrative candidates yearly. The average cost of implementing the training program in the school district in this study during the 2008-2009 school year was approximately $4,493. This amount was relatively inexpensive considering participants attended 12 full-day trainings in addition to professional development team meetings five times throughout the school year. Furthermore, by utilizing district initiatives for training purposes, program costs were absorbed (as in-kind contributions).

Another finding was the tension between program developers and program stakeholders about the amount of theory that should be incorporated within the program versus the amount of technical training participants should receive. This tension was at the core of the discontent expressed by many stakeholders of the program. Participants communicated that they wanted the training to give them skills in executing the technical aspects of the job. Yet, program developers wanted to simultaneously build participants' technical capacities and their adaptive leadership abilities. Participants and some stakeholders did not value the extent of reflection that was provided by the program, as they felt a "grow your own" program's purpose was to enhance technical skills.

Another significant finding was the need for authentic, substantive internships for secondary administrators. All of the candidates that participated in the internship program within the Northwest School District completed a university internship program for their initial administrative licensure. The state in which this study was conducted did not require a full-time internship. Candidates generally completed the requirements of their university internship under the supervision of a school-based administrator and a university supervisor. These internship opportunities did not prepare candidates for the principalship in the Northwest School District and the Northwest School District attempted to give candidates a more authentic internship experience. Although the internship provided by the Northwest School District was not deemed substantive, the 4-weeks participants spent leading a building was more robust than the typical internship that universities offered. Participants in the Northwest School District described the internship as "loosy-goosy," indicating a need for support in structuring the activities that are completed during the internship experience.

IMPLICATIONS AND RECOMMENDATIONS FOR PRACTICE

The findings from this study present several implications for school districts interested in creating grow your own principal training programs, state departments of education interested in supporting the development of principal training programs, graduate schools of education, and the school district involved in this study.

Recommendations for School Districts Interested in Creating "Grow Your Own" Programs

School districts concerned with increasing the quantity or quality of their principal candidates should consider developing their own district level "grow your own" programs. The Northwest School District, as well as other school districts, have increased the quantity of potential principal applicants in school districts. These programs have also shown promise in increasing the quality of principal candidates, though the degree to which programs have increased quality varies from district to district based upon the program design (Miracle, 2006; Morrison, 2005).

It is essential for a school district that is considering developing a "grow your own" program to clearly define a shared vision and mission for the program. It is also essential to identify clear, objective performance-based outcomes for participants within the program. Once outcomes are defined, a system should be established to determine how growth will be objectively measured and feedback will be provided to administrative candidates. In small districts, it would be beneficial to collaborate with university personnel to identify clear standards and evaluation methods to ensure that outcomes of the program are effectively and objectively evaluated. "Grow your own" programs need systemwide leadership as it relates to both the vision and purpose of the programs and the resources associated with the program. The goals and outcomes of the program should be directly linked to school district's strategic plan to ensure that it is a funding priority for the school system. As was the case with the Northwest School District, the costs of "grow your own" programs can remain relatively stable, but it is important for a system that is planning on implementing a "grow your own" program to have a well-designed strategic plan with realistic budget costs in the development of the program. A clearly articulated strategic plan is essential to effective communication about the program in all its facets to stakeholders.

In considering the development of a district level principal program, school districts should utilize a collaborative process to design, develop, and implement their programs. Principals should be on the design team and in the continuous improvement process as they are the primary trainers of administrative candidates. These programs can do much to build the capacity of both the administrative participants and administrative trainers. This would acknowledge the fact that the difference between a principal trainer and a participant may be a matter of a few months. With principal shortages accelerating, this phenomenon will occur more frequently. School systems can utilize the expertise of experienced administrative candidates to serve as trainers and presenters. One potential challenge of many school district training programs is that experienced administrative candidates, if they do not assume a principalship immediately, do not receive support or attention. In the Northwest School District, for example, only five administrative candidates are considered for an internship as an AP3. In a large school district with over 80 assistant principals with three or more years of experience, opportunities should be offered for experienced assistant principals that are strong to share their expertise and be acknowledged for their contribution to developing candidates. It is an inexpensive way to give principal candidates with experience opportunities to hone their leadership skills and train candidates on concrete topics. The program would then be viewed as an ongoing professional development program for principals and experienced assistant principals to continue to learn and develop their skills while supporting others. In return, the school district could provide free training to presenters to continue their development.

School systems interested in developing "grow your own" programs should evaluate their own local issues and concerns and develop the content of the program collaboratively to ensure the program meets the needs of participants and the school system. During the design of the program, there should be frequent opportunities for program designers and implementers to receive feedback on implementation. Feedback opportunities should occur more than once per year, and districtwide support should be given to ensure trainers are properly trained.

A school district seeking to develop a district level development program should evaluate existing training opportunities within their district. Once a clear vision of the essential skills is established, and those skills are communicated to all stakeholders, systemwide leadership is needed from various offices within the school district to orchestrate a systematic approach to supporting administrative candidates. This is a cost effective way to develop programs utilizing existing school system resources. The costs of developing a principal development program can be reduced by utilizing the resources and expertise of offices and school personnel within the school district. School personnel should support the outcomes of the training program by serving as guest trainers during the work day. One key to success is ensuring that "silos" are not allowed to exist in which the resources of the system are not effectively utilized to benefit the skill development of administrative candidates. A strategic plan for supporting skills should be developed to ensure all training is aligned with the vision and mission of the program.

School districts seeking to develop a "grow your own" program should develop a system to ensure that the district's best principals serve as the building-level trainers of principal candidates. This will require school district leadership as administrative candidates would frequently move to different schools for different learning experiences. If building the capacity of future principals is a priority, it should be done with trainers who are willing to be trained and willing to train others.

School districts that seek to develop a "grow your own" program should explore job sharing as a way to increase the amount of time participants experience job-embedded training through an internship. Principals at one level of schooling can replace the assistant principals at other levels of schooling within the district to learn skills at different schooling levels. For example, an elementary principal can assume the role of middle school assistant principal to release the middle school assistant principal to serve as principal of a middle school. This interchange has the ability to increase the skills of both administrators if it is structured in a manner that allows for critical reflection and experiences in different aspects of the job.

Recommendations for State Departments of Education

State departments of education should support school districts by funding fully released internships in secondary administrative positions. Researchers have identified the internship as a significant experience for administrative candidates (Bass, 1990; Cappasso & Daresh, 2001; Creighton, 2001; Wilmore, 2002). Recent studies have found that the internship program in graduate schools of education can be inadequate (Bottoms, O'Neill, & Frye, 2005; Murphy & Vriesenga, 2006). Full-time year-long internships can be supported by state departments of education to ensure that administrative candidates receive authentic administrative experiences. School districts can receive funds to provide authentic internships to administrative candidates. The funding of fully released internships should be based upon a competitive application process in which candidates demonstrate competency and experiences aligned with the rigorous demands of the position. State departments of education should require school districts to describe how they will support administrative candidates based upon effective practices, including providing candidates with an experienced mentor, providing reflective opportunities, providing cohort learning opportunities for candidates, and providing clear performance based standards for candidates, and continuous review of program implementation. This funding incentive will increase school districts' likelihood of evaluation of their programs and compliance.

In addition, state departments of education should allow school districts that develop their own principal development programs to alternatively license administrative candidates if school districts fund year-long internships for candidates who may have advanced degrees but have not gone through an accredited graduate school of education. School districts, facing a shortage of qualified applicants, should be able to seek licensure abilities if they can provide evidence of objectively supporting and training their own administrative cohorts. The Mid-Atlantic state in which this study was conducted presently requires administrative candidates to take the School Leadership Series test to become licensed to become a principal after candidates initial licensure is received through an accredited university program. The Northwest School District feels candidates are not prepared for the realities of the principalship after achieving their licensure, so by allowing school systems to license administrators, it will serve as an incentive for districts to develop more comprehensive programs.

State departments of education can provide funding to districts to hire mentors to work with new administrative candidates. Mentor administrators have been identified as having a positive influence on new administrative candidates. As of 2006, roughly half of the nation's states have implemented requirements for the mentoring of administrators (Wallace Foundation, 2007). Funding by state departments of education can increase the rate of school districts supporting administrative candidates with mentors. There was a clear benefit described by candidates in having principal consultants work with them as they reflected upon the challenges of educational administration.

State departments of education can also offer training for principal mentors. Principals may be effective leaders, but training others to lead requires a different set of skills. Principals need support and training to effectively work with administrative candidates. State departments of education could offer regional trainings to school districts that developed mentoring programs. This would serve as an incentive to school districts that have developed mentor relationships and it would encourage other districts to establish mentoring opportunities.

Recommendations for Graduate Schools of Education

Graduate schools of education can provide support to school districts attempting to develop district-level principal training programs by assisting districts to ensure that their programs are aligned with best practices noted in research findings. The district in this study had a full-time director of leadership development, who researched, designed, and implemented the program. A partnership with local universities will ensure that leadership development programs are not based solely upon the efforts and expertise of one individual in a school district.

Graduate schools of education can also work with local school districts in providing objective measures to evaluate progress on identified outcomes. To limit the subjectivity of performance-based assessments, rubrics could be developed and sent to university evaluation staff for objective feedback. The school district in this study, and research findings from previous research (Miracle, 2006; Morrison, 2005), found that "grow your own" programs are not receiving the critical evaluation and feedback that they need to continuously improve. One challenge may be that many districts do not have evaluation/accountability departments that are capable of effectively evaluating the effectiveness of programs. This is an area where there are opportunities for graduate schools of education to partner with local school systems to ensure programs are receiving the critical feedback they need to improve.

Graduate schools of education can work with local school districts to systematically provide administrative candidates with significant opportunities to reflect through exposing administrative candidates to leadership theory. An understanding of critical theory and its application to new situations is crucial for administrator effectiveness. The reality of the principalship is that new challenges and new situations arise daily. It is unrealistic to assume that any training program can provide a "cook book" of technical skills that will ensure administrative candidates' success. As was the case in this study, many administrative participants do not understand the significance of "moving to the balcony" and reflecting to acquire new learning. School districts, which may be limited by human resources, may not have the capacity to effectively research and train administrative candidates on current, relevant theories of leadership using an interdisciplinary approach. Partnering with local school districts to provide critical theory to administrative candidates as they apply theories in practical settings would enhance administrative training and reduce the time school districts needed to address these issues.

While not perfect, Northwest's program was successful in developing a multiyear, tiered system at a reasonable per-participant cost by relying largely on existing personnel to deliver the program. As noted in this study, there are many facets to consider when implementing such programs. Further, given the variability in district size and resources, there are key roles for stakeholders outside the district to play in implementing these programs. Systematic evaluation can both strengthen such programs as well as provide valuable "lessons learned" to Northwest and other districts interested in creating grow your own programs.

NOTE

1.   All personnel and district names have been changed to protect confidentiality.

REFERENCES

Baitland, B. F. (1992). *An evaluation of an experiential school principal preparation program at the University of Houston.* Doctoral dissertation. (UMI No. 9225036)

Bass, G. R. (1990, November). The practitioner's role in preparing successful school administrators. *NASSP Bulletin, 74*(529), 27-30.

Bottoms, G., O'Neill, K., & Frye, B. (2005). The principal internship: How can we get it right? Retrieved from www.wallacefoundation.org

Bottoms, G., O'Neill, K. Frye, B., & Jacobson, A. (2004). *Progress being made in getting a quality leader in every school.* Atlanta, GA: Southern Regional Education Board. Retrieved from http://sreb.org/main/Goals/Publications/04E12_Quality_Leader.pdf

The Broad Foundation and Fordham Foundation. (2003). *Better leaders for America's schools: A manifesto.* Retrieved from http://www.edexcellence.net/detail/news.cfm?news_id=1

Browne-Ferrigno, T. (2001, November). *Preparing school leaders: Case study summary and implications.* (ERIC Document Reproduction Services No. ED465226)

Capasso, R. L., & Daresh, J. C. (2001). *The school administrator internship handbook: Leading, mentoring, and participating in the internship program.* Thousand Oaks, CA: Corwin Press.

Copeland, M. A. (2001, March). The myth of superprincipal. *Phi Delta Kappan, 82*(7), 528-540.

Cox, H. S. (1998). Effectiveness of principal preparation in Florida as perceived by selected superintendents, first-year principals and other key informants. Doctoral dissertation. (UMI No. 9838576)

Creighton, T. B. (2001). *Towards a leadership practice field: An antidote to an ailing internship experience*. (ERIC Document Reproduction Services No. ED 458698)

Dodson, R. (2006). The effectiveness of principal training and formal principal mentoring programs. Doctoral dissertation. (UMI No. 3222298)

Edmonds, R. (1979). Effective schools for the urban poor. *Educational Leadership, 32*, 15-27.

Educational Research Services. (2000). *The principal, keystone of a high achieving school: Attracting and keeping the leaders we need*. Washington, DC: National Association of Elementary School Principals and National Association of Secondary School Principals.

Gall, M. D., Borg, W. R., & Gall, J. P. (1996). *Educational research: An introduction*. White Plains, NY: Longman.

Hallinger, P. (1992). The evolving role of American principals: From managerial to instructional to transformational leaders. *Journal of Educational Administration, 30*(3), 35-49.

Jackson, B., & Kelley C. (2002, April). Exceptional and innovative programs in educational leadership. *Educational Administration Quarterly, 38*, 192-211.

Leithwood, K., Louis, K. S., Anderson, S., & Wahlstrom, K. (2004). How leadership influences student learning. Retrieved from http://www.wallacefoundation.org/KnowledgeCenter/KnowledgeTopics/EducationLeadership/HowLeadershipInfluencesStudentLearning.htm

National Commission on Excellence in Educational Administration (1987). *Leaders for America's schools*. Tempe, AZ: University Council for Educational Administration.

Levine, A. (2005). *Educating school leaders*. New York, NY: The Education Schools Project.

Maryland Task Force on the Principalship. (2000). *Recommendations for redefining the role of the principal; recruiting, retaining, and rewarding principals; and improving their preparation and development*. Baltimore, MD: Maryland State Board of Education.

Mercado, L. P. (2002). *The secondary principalship academy. A critical ethnography of the Houston Independent School District and the University of Houston's innovative principal preparation program*. Doctoral dissertation. (UMI No. 3067773)

Milstein, M., & Krueger, J.A. (1997). Improving educational administration preparation programs: What we have learned over the past decade. *Peabody Journal of Education, 72*(2), 100-116.

Miracle, T. L. (2006). *An analysis of a district-level aspiring principals training program*. Doctoral dissertation. (UMI No. 3228666)

Morrison, H. (2005). *A critical evaluation of a school system's effort to develop and implement a grow your own principal preparation program*. Doctoral dissertation. (UMI No. 3178557)

Murphy, J. (1990). Improving the preparation of school administrators: The national policy board's story. *Journal of Education Policy, 5*(2), 181-186.

Murphy, J. (1994). *Transformational change and the evolving role of the principal: Early empirical evidence*. (ERIC Document Reproduction Services No. ED374520)

Murphy, J. (2002). Reculturing the profession of educational leadership: New blueprints. *Educational Administration Quarterly, 38*(2), 176-191.

Murphy, J., & Forsyth, P.E. (1999). *Educational Administration: A decade of reform.* Thousand Oaks, CA: Corwin Press.

Murphy, J., & Hallinger, P. (1992). The principalship in an era of transformation. *Journal of Educational Administration*, 2(3), 77-89.

Murphy, M., & Vriesenga, M. (2006, April). Research on school leadership preparation in the United States: An analysis. *School Leadership and Management*, 26, 183-195.

Newman, C. A. (2004). *Interim evaluation of the UNT/Dallas Public School Leadership Development Program: A working model.* Doctoral dissertation. (UMI No. 3126581)

Portin, B. S. (1997). *Complexity and capacity: A survey of principal role change in Washington state.* (ERIC Document Reproduction Services No. ED414 624)

Portin, B. S., Shen, J., & Williams, R. C. (1998, December). The changing principalship and its impact: Voices from principals. *National Association of Secondary School Principals Bulletin*, 82(602), 1-4.

Stufflebeam, D. L. (2000). The CIPP model for evaluation. In D. L. Stufflebeam, G. F. Madaus, & T. Kellaghan (Eds.), *Evaluation models* (2nd ed., pp. 279-317). Boston, MA: Kluwer Academic.

Tirozzi, G. N. (2001, February). The artistry of leadership: The evolving role of secondary school principal. *Phi Delta Kappan*, 82(6), 434-440.

Wallace Foundation. (2007, March). *Getting principal mentoring right: Lessons from the field.* Retrieved December 7, 2007, from www.wallacefoundation.org

Wallace Foundation. (2012, June). *Principals in the Pipeline: Districts construct a framework to develop school leaders.* Retrieved July 1, 2012, from www.wallacefoundation.org

Waters, T., Marzano, R. J., & McNulty, B. (2003). *Balanced leadership: What 30 years of research tells us about the effect of leadership on student achievement.* Aurora, CO: Mid-Continent Research for Education and Learning.

Whitaker, K. S. (2003). Principal role changes and influence on principal recruitment and selection: An international perspective. *Journal of Educational Administration*, 41(1), 37-54.

Wilmore, E. L. (2002). *Principal leadership: Applying the new Education Leadership Constituent Council (ELCC) standards.* Thousand Oaks, CA: Corwin Press.

Witziers, B., Bosker, R.J., & Kruger, M.L. (2003). Educational leadership and student achievement: The elusive search for an association. *Education Administration Quarterly*, 39(3), 398-425.

CHAPTER 4

PRINCIPALS' KNOWLEDGE OF SPECIAL EDUCATION POLICIES AND PROCEDURES

Does it Matter in Leadership?

Lindsay Jesteadt and Meredith Mountford

ABSTRACT

This study is an investigation of the knowledge of Florida school principals in the area of special education policies and procedures. A survey was designed to establish the method by which school principals purport to have learned the majority of special education policies and procedures. Social justice as defined by Adams, Bell, and Griffin (1997) and ethical reasoning in educational leadership, developed and defined by Shapiro and Stefkovich (2005) were chosen as the conceptual frameworks that guided the design and analysis of the study. These underlying sets of ideas were used to help recognize the many inequalities that have hindered education for a variety of students, including those with disabilities (Lashley, 2007). Findings from this study demonstrate the level of knowledge practicing administrators in Florida possess, the methods by which they acquired that knowledge, and the need for this knowledge under new state mandated reform initiatives.

Research in Learning and Teaching in Educational Leadership
pp. 85–125

85

School leadership has changed considerably over the years due to federal policies that have been put in place during this era of great public school accountability. This accountability system focuses on the educational performance of all students, including students with disabilities (Lashley, 2007). Keith (2011) affirmed:

> Since current mandates assure that the programs and services for children with disabilities are in absolute compliance with the law, building principals absolutely must be knowledgeable and prepared to supervise the array of special education services within their schools and to make decisions regarding best practices. (p. 124)

While the overall objective of principal leadership training programs is to prepare future school leaders, commonly accepted leadership standards such as The National Council for Accreditation in Teacher Education or The Interstate School Leaders Licensure Consortium (ISLLC) standards rarely focus specifically on the knowledge necessary for principals to work effectively with students who exhibit learning or behavioral disabilities, despite the fact most school principals will lead in schools that include a portion of these students within the school population (Crockett, 2002; DiPaola & Tschannen-Moran, 2003; Doyle, 2001). Research has suggested deficits may exist in administrator accreditation programs in regards to diverse learners, exceptionality, and disability (DiPaola & Tschannen-Moran, 2003). With this lack of knowledge specifically related to special education policies and procedures, it is likely many administrators are going into the field unprepared to deal with the everyday realities of educating students with disabilities (Aspedon, 1992; Dickenson, Knopp, & Fauske, 2003; DiPaola & Walther-Thomas, 2003; Doyle, 2001; McClard-Bertrand & Bratberg, 2007; Potter & Hulsey, 2001; Smith & Colon, 1998).

PURPOSE OF THE STUDY

The purpose of this study was to assess the knowledge school principals have in the area of special education policies and procedures and to establish the method (i.e., college coursework, district in-services, self-taught, on the job) by which school principals purport to have learned special education policies and procedures specifically related to the six principles of the 2004 Individuals with Disabilities Education Improvement Act (IDEA). Data generated from the principals' knowledge of special education policies and procedures was then compared to (a) the amount of special education coursework taken during the principal's formal education, (b) the method by which school principals learned the majority of their knowledge of special education policies and procedures, (c) past teaching experience in the field of special education, (d) school enrollment, and (e) types of communities (i.e., rural, suburban, and urban).

RESEARCH QUESTIONS

In order to address the purpose of this study, a conceptual framework along with the following overarching research questions and subquestions guided the design and analysis of data in this quantitative study.

1. What knowledge do Florida principals possess in the areas of special education policies and procedures, as defined by the Individuals with Disabilities Education Improvement Act of 2004?
2. What was the primary method (i.e., college coursework, district in-services, self-learning, on the job) by which principals purport to have learned the majority of special education policies and procedures?

The research subquestions were as follows:

(a) Do principals who receive formal training (i.e., any level of college coursework in any program area) in special education have a greater level of overall knowledge in the area of special education policies and procedures than principals who did not receive formal training in special education?
(b) Is there a relationship between the principals' knowledge levels in the area of special education policies and procedures, as defined by the six principles of IDEA 2004, and the method by which they received the majority of their knowledge for each area?
(c) Do principals who have prior teaching experience in the field of special education have a greater level of overall knowledge in the area of special education policies and procedures than principals who did not have prior teaching experience in the field of special education?
(d) Is the level of overall knowledge in the area of special education policies and procedures similar among principals across different school sizes, as measured by school enrollment?
(e) Is the level of overall knowledge in the area of special education policies and procedures similar among principals across community types (i.e., rural, suburban, and urban)?

CONCEPTUAL FRAMEWORK:
SOCIAL JUSTICE AND ETHICAL REASONING

Social justice as defined by Adams, Bell, and Griffin (1997) and ethical reasoning in educational leadership, developed and defined by Shapiro and Stefkovich (2005) were chosen as the conceptual framework with which to guide the design and assist in the interpretation of the findings of the study. These underlying sets of ideas were used to help recognize the many inequalities that have hindered education for a variety of students, including those with disabilities (Lashley, 2007). The following sections discuss the lenses of social justice and ethical reasoning which were used to guide the analysis of the data and assist in the interpretation of the findings.

Social Justice

The term social justice has been defined as many different ways as there are authors who have written about it. McKenzie et al. (2008) argues for a nonessentialized definition of social justice, where there is not one meaning, nor can it be universally applied in every situation in the same way. Bogotch (2002a) asserts that social justice is a social construction and there are no fixed or predictable meanings of social justice prior to actually engaging in educational leadership practices. Drawing on the philosophies of John Dewey, who contends that a truly democratic society concerns itself essentially with social justice, the research makes it clear that creating equal opportunities and eliminating injustices must become a priority in our communities as well as our schools (Aronson, 2004; Larson & Ovando, 2001; Marshall & Gerstl-Pepin, 2005; Rosener, 1990; Young, Mountford, & Skrla, 2006). For the purpose of this research, the researchers utilized the definition of social justice by Adams et al. (1997) who discussed social justice as both process oriented and goal oriented. Further they point out both the process and goals are inextricably linked to fair and just resource distribution:

> It means full and equal participation of all groups in a society that is mutually shaped to meet their needs. Social justice includes a vision of society in which the distribution of resources is equitable and all members are physically and psychologically safe and secure. We envision a society in which individuals are both self determining (able to develop their full capacities), and interdependent (capable of interacting democratically with others). (p. 240)

Ethical Reasoning: Justice, Care, Critique, and Profession

A second conceptual framework, developed by Shapiro and Stefkovich (2005) for ethical reasoning in educational leadership, looks at the four approaches to ethical analysis: an ethic of justice, an ethic of care, an ethic of critique, and an ethic of the profession. Lashley (2007) suggested these four approaches could be used to

> guide the decision making of principals as they confront unfamiliar and complex dilemmas in their schools.... These perspectives pose different questions for administrators to consider as they make decisions that hold them accountable to stakeholders and responsible for the children they serve. (p. 182)

Viewing ethical dilemmas through an ethic of justice, "one may ask questions related to the rule of law and the more abstract concepts of fairness, equity and justice" (Shapiro & Stefkovich, 2005, p. 12). This area may include the issues of equality and equity, the fairness of rules, laws and policies, and rights of individuals versus the greater good.

> Overall, the ethic of justice considers questions such as: Is there a law, right, or policy that relates to a particular case? If there is a law, right, or policy, should it be enforced? And if there is not a law, right, or policy, should there be one? (Shapiro & Stefkovich, 2005, p. 13)

With regard to ethical reasoning of principals working with special education students, Lashley (2007) adds that a school principal

> must understand the rights inherent in IDEA and why they are in place. He or she must also know the legal and policy requirements of the law, as well as understand the historical and educational contexts that have led to these requirements. (p. 184)

Growing out of the ethic of justice, the ethic of care, which is associated with feminist theory, requires leaders to consider the multiple voices in the decision making process (Shapiro & Stefkovich, 2005).

> This ethic asks that individuals consider the consequences of their decisions and actions. It asks them to consider questions such as: Who will benefit from what I decide? Who will be hurt by my actions? What are the long-term effects of a decision I make today? (Shapiro & Stefkovich, 2005, p. 16)

The ethic of critique, which is inherent in critical theory, is aimed at awakening educators to inequities in society and, in particular, in the schools (Shapiro & Stefkovich, 2005). Educators are asked to deal with the hard questions regarding social class, race, gender, and disabilities. The ethic of critique focuses on questions regarding who makes the laws, rules, or policies; who benefits from the laws, rules, or policies; who holds the power; and who are the silenced voices (Shapiro & Stefkovich, 2005).

> The disaggregation of performance data required under [No Child Left Behind] raises issues about students who have been historically undercon-sidered in school decision making. When principals use data to inform their decisions, they cannot ignore the achievement gaps that they discover. (Lashley, 2007, p. 185)

Finally, the ethic of the profession looks at providing training in ethics for school leaders. This preparation could "enable a prospective principal or superintendent to develop attitudes, beliefs, knowledge, and skills associated with competence in moral reasoning" (Greenfield, 1993, p. 285). Greenfield believes a failure to develop this competence in school administrators represents a failure to serve the children we are obligated to serve: "In educational administration, we believe that if there is a moral imperative for the profession, it is to serve the 'best interests of the stu-dent [including those with disabilities]'" (Shapiro & Stefkovich, 2005, p. 26). The ethic of the profession addresses the question, "What should I do based on the best interests of the students who may be diverse in their composition and needs?" (Lashley, 2007, p. 186).

The conceptual frame described above was used to guide the study as well as interpret the results. In addition, several earlier studies focused on the knowledge principals hold about special education, how or where they attained that knowledge, principal leadership development programs, and school leadership standards guiding universities and school districts in preparing school leaders were also reviewed to inform this study.

REVIEW OF LITERATURE

Research consistently finds most school principals do not have sufficient knowledge in special education. This lack of knowledge is most often said to be a function of university preparation programs and school district professional development programs prioritizing curriculum related to instructional, operational, and managerial leadership knowledge, skills, and dispositions over their knowledge of policies and procedures for spe-cialized populations (Aspedon, 1992; Dickenson et al., 2003; DiPaola & Walther-Thomas, 2003; Doyle, 2001; McClard-Bertrand & Bratberg, 2007; Potter & Hulsey, 2001; Smith & Colon, 1998). The research demon-strates that despite a national rhetoric of training school leaders toward equality and social justice, principals most often lack the background experiences and training necessary to understand the various legal or equity issues associated with special education or to create programs in which students with disabilities can experience success (DiPaola & Walther-Thomas, 2003; Doyle, 2001; McClard-Bertrand & Bratberg, 2007). The following sections review findings from previous studies that investigated the knowledge level of principals related to various aspects of special education, their attitudes toward students with special needs, and the common forms of training. Following the review of studies related to principals' knowledge level of special education, various standards that drive the curriculum common to many leadership development programs are discussed at both the national and the state level for the state that was the site of the study, Florida.

Principals' Knowledge of Special Education

The findings from a series of studies focused on principals' attitudes toward special education (Dickenson et al., 2003), principals' perceptions of their knowledge of special education (Aspedon, 1992), and what principals know versus what they need to know about special education (McClard-Bertrand & Bratberg, 2007) indicated a lack of educational training and preparation in dealing with students with disabilities. One finding showed over 72% of principals surveyed had little exposure to persons with disabilities and over 85% of the principals felt formal training in special education was needed (Aspedon, 1992). These findings suggest such a lack of training and exposure to specific populations of students only hinder the knowledge necessary to be a successful school leader.

McClard-Bertrand and Bratberg (2007) found that principals' lack of knowledge is most significant in the areas of testing and evaluation procedures used to determine eligibility for special education students. Additionally, they found weaknesses in principals' aptitude in understanding the differences between IDEA and Section 504 of the 1973 Vocational-Rehabilitation Act, as well as in the area of funding to determine special education appropriations. Their study concluded more extensive formal training in special education was necessary if school leaders are to have the knowledge necessary to operate successful special education programs in their schools.

Studies soliciting the perceptions of principals regarding the strength of their own training found the majority of principals believe they did not receive professional development training specifically on special education from neither their school district nor their administrative preparation programs and reported feeling inadequate with the level of knowledge they possessed to deal with special education issues in the schools they led (Dickenson et al., 2003). In short, "most principals lack the course work and field experience needed to lead local efforts to create learning environments that emphasize academic success for students with disabilities" (DiPaola & Walther-Thomas, 2003, p. 11).

Due to the lack of knowledge school leaders possess in the area of special education, many principals are entering the field with feelings of inadequacy and a sense of being overwhelmed by issues associated with special education (Doyle, 2001; Potter & Hulsey, 2001; Smith & Colon, 1998). Yet with the No Child Left Behind Act and the reauthorization of IDEA, school leaders are expected to be instructional leaders for all programs, including special education programs. This expectation leads administrators to feel unprepared and inundated (Doyle, 2001). Principals do not consider themselves well equipped for the varied responsibilities that operating a successful special education program entails (Potter & Hulsey, 2001). Some researchers go as far as to suggest one of the most complex and difficult educational tasks for administrators is being able to understand and implement effective special education programs (Smith & Colon, 1998). However, since many administrators feel insufficient with their knowledge in this area they delegate the responsibility to someone else who is likely just as unprepared.

Administrative support in dealing with special education is crucial for the success of special education programs (Keyes, Hanley-Maxwell, & Capper, 1999). One of the studies reviewed suggested what principals most desperately need is a firm foundation in the knowledge of special education programs, policies, and procedures. Krajewski and Krajewski (2000) found that principals must have a broad knowledge base about students with disabilities and develop a school-based plan for success in which the principal is an active member. Those administrators who obtained special training or professional development related to educating students with disabilities indicated such training and background is beneficial to their leadership role in special education at the school level (Patterson, Marshall, & Bowling, 2000). It appears as though administrators who have a clear understanding of the needs of students' with disabilities, IDEA, and the instructional challenges special education teachers face are better prepared to provide the support special education teachers need to be successful educators (DiPaola & Walther-Thomas, 2003).

McKenzie et al. (2008) analyzed the implications of socially just schooling when principals demonstrate a lack of knowledge of special education policy and procedures. They concluded, "preparation programs for social justice must teach prospective principals how to recognize structures that pose barriers to students' progress and create proactive structures and systems of support for all students at the macro and micro levels" (p. 126).

Similarly, Capper, Theoharis, & Sebastian (2006) call for an increased attention to assessing preparation programs and how they prepare leaders for social justice.

While it is well documented in the research that school leaders need to be prepared to be effective advocates for all students, the research also recognizes many school leaders have not acquired the knowledge necessary to provide leadership to students and teachers in special education (Aspedon, 1992; Dickenson et al., 2003; DiPaola & Walther-Thomas, 2003; Doyle, 2001; McClard-Bertrand & Bratberg, 2007; Potter & Hulsey, 2001; Smith & Colon, 1998). As Secretary Duncan (2010) acknowledged in his speech on the 35th anniversary of IDEA, "For all the progress, we can all agree that we haven't completely fulfilled the promise of IDEA. Our children continue to face prejudices and lingering roadblocks" (para. 1).

ISLLC Standards for Educational Leadership

"Since the release of the 1987 report of the National Commission on Excellence in Educational Administration, *Leaders for America's Schools,* considerable attention has been devoted to finding ways to improve the quality of leadership in our schools and school systems" (Murphy, Yff, & Shipman, 2000, p. 17). In 1996, the ISLLC, which comprises state and professional associations, published a comprehensive set of standards for school leaders. The standards were designed to eliminate the confusion and create conformity among educational leadership programs (Green, 2001). These standards "provide[d] the means to shift the metric of school administration from management to educational leadership and from administration to learning while linking management and behavioral science knowledge to the larger goal of student learning" (Murphy, 2005, p. 166).

Through the years, there has been much criticism of the ISLLC Standards for School Leaders (Boeckmann & Dickinson, 2001; Bogotch, 2002b; Creighton, 2002; English, 2001; Foster, 2003; Hess, 2003; Leithwood & Steinbach, 2003). One critic felt the ISLLC standards face the imminent possibility of extinction (Leithwood & Steinbach, 2003); while others believed they will only add to the predictable pattern of failed reform efforts (Bogotch, 2002b). Murphy (2005) has responded to these and additional criticisms by exclaiming, "the standards are exactly what they claim to be—what practitioners and researchers have told us are critical aspects of effective leadership" (p. 41).

In 2008, the ISLLC Standards were revised "to provide a framework for policy creation, training program performance, life-long career development and system support" (The Council of Chief State School Officers, 2008, p. 11). The following principles set the direction and priorities during the development of the Educational Leadership Policy Standards, ISLLC 2008:

1. reflect the centrality of student learning;
2. acknowledge the changing role of the school leader;
3. recognize the collaborative nature of school leadership;
4. improve the quality of the profession;
5. inform performance-based systems of assessment and evaluation for school leaders;
6. demonstrate integration and coherence; and
7. advance access, opportunity, and empowerment for all members of the school community (The Council of Chief State School Officers, 2008, p. 8).

On December 12, 2007, the Educational Leadership Policy Standards: ISLLC 2008 was adopted by the National Policy Board for Educational Administration. The ISLLC Standards read as follows:

1. An education leader promotes the success of every student by facilitating the development, articulation, implementation, and stewardship of a vision of learning that is shared and supported by all stakeholders.
2. An education leader promotes the success of every student by advocating, nurturing, and sustaining a school culture and instructional program conducive to student learning and staff professional growth.
3. An education leader promotes the success of every student by ensuring management of the organization, operation, and resources for a safe, efficient, and effective learning environment.
4. An education leader promotes the success of every student by collaborating with faculty and community members, responding to diverse community interests and needs, and mobilizing community resources.
5. An education leader promotes the success of every student by acting with integrity, fairness, and in an ethical manner.
6. An education leader promotes the success of every student by understanding, responding to, and influencing the political, social, economic, legal, and cultural context (p. 14).

ISLLC standards have created the framework that assisted in the development of the Florida principal leadership standards, William Cecil Golden school leadership development program, and programs for both preservice school leadership and in-service school leaders.

Florida's Principal Leadership Standards

Prior to the induction of the Florida Principal Leadership Standards, the Florida Legislature had established the Management Training Act. This act worked to create a trilevel support system: state, regional and district, to guarantee that principals have the skills and background that are crucial in providing effective leadership (Office of Program Policy Analysis and Government Accountability, 2000). The Management Training Act specified 19 competencies for school principals, which were acquired through university and district programs. These competency areas were (a) proactive orientation, (b) decisiveness, (c) commitment to school mission, (d) interpersonal search, (e) information search, (f) concept formation, (g) conceptual flexibility, (h) managing interaction, (i) persuasiveness, (j) concern for image, (k) tactical adaptability, (l) achievement motivation, (m) management control, (n) developmental orientation, (o) organizational ability, (p) delegation, (q) self-presentation, (r) written communication, and (s) organizational sensitivity. In 1999, the Florida Legislature was unsure if the act was successful in providing the necessary skills and knowledge base for school leaders. They directed that the Office of Program Policy Analysis and Government Accountability, in consultation with the Department of Education, "conduct a comprehensive review of the Management Training Act by January 1, 2000, and make recommendations for the act's repeal, revision, or reauthorization" (Office of Program Policy Analysis and Government Accountability, 2000, p. 1).

The Florida Department of Education Regulation 6A-5.080 outlines the Florida Principal Leadership Standards that were approved in April of 2005. In an attempt to foster specific abilities and skills in potential school leaders, ten standards were created in which a person must demonstrate his or her competency levels. These ten standards were split into three broad categories: instructional leadership, operational leadership, and school leadership. The instructional leadership standards were (a) instructional leadership, (b) managing the learning environment, and (c) learning, accountability, and assessment. The operational leadership standards were (a) decision making strategies, (b) technology, (c) human resource development, and (d) ethical leadership. The school leadership standards were (a) vision, (b) community and stakeholder partnerships, and (c) diversity. In addition, each of the ten standards had key indicators/ attributes that correlated to three specific levels of school leaders: entry, career, and high performing.

William Cecil Golden School Leadership Development Program

In the time since these standards were last approved, the William Cecil Golden School Leadership Development Program was established by the 2006 Florida Legislature. The goal of this program is "to provide a high quality, competency-based, customized, comprehensive and coordinated statewide professional development system for current and emerging school leaders" (Florida Department of Education, 2006, para. 1). The program uses a collaborative network of state and national leadership development organizations to support the needs of current and developing principals.

In June of 2007, the Florida State Department of Education Regulation 6A-5.081 was passed to ensure that preservice school leadership programs as well as in-service school leaders are of high quality as required in Section 1012.986, F.S. This rule lays out the foundation of requirements for approval of two levels of school leadership programs (Florida State Board of Education, 2007). These two levels include programs offered by both Florida postsecondary institutions as well as the public school districts.

On September 13, 2011 there was a rule development conference call with the Florida Department of Education. The purpose of this rule development was to review the existing standards that Florida school leaders must demonstrate in preparation programs and in personnel evaluations as well as to propose revised standards that align fully with the contemporary research on effective school leadership. On October 3, 2011, the proposed leadership standards were created. Four domains of effective leadership were identified: student achievement, instructional leadership, organizational leadership, and professional and ethical behavior. Under these four domains, ten leadership standards were created: student learning results, student learning as a priority, instructional plan implementation, faculty development, learning environment, decision making, leadership development, school management, communication, and professional and ethical behaviors. Presently, none of the standards for school leaders address issues concerning students with disabilities although proponents of the latest set of standards argue knowledge of special education policy and procedures falls under ethical behaviors but is not explicit in the standard.

The purpose of this study was to assess the knowledge school principals have in the area of special education policies and procedures and to establish the method (i.e., college coursework, district in-services, self-taught, on the job) by which school principals purport to have learned special education policies and procedures specifically related to the six principles of the Individuals with Disabilities Education Improvement Act (IDEA) 2004. Data generated from the principals' knowledge of special education policies and procedures was then compared to (a) the amount of special education coursework taken during the principals' formal education, (b) the method by which school principals learned the majority of their knowledge of special education policies and procedures, (c) past teaching experience in the field of special education, (d) school enrollment, and (e) types of communities (i.e., rural, suburban, and urban). The following sections of the chapter will outline the research design and methods used to conduct the study.

RESEARCH DESIGN AND METHODS

This quantitative study was designed utilizing a two-part survey to collect background/demographic information, level of special education knowledge, and sources of specified special education knowledge from all traditional Florida public school principals. The first section of the survey included respondent background and school demographic information. The second section consisted of 12 hypothetical scenarios based on the six major principles of special education within IDEA 2004: zero reject, nondiscriminatory evaluation, least restrictive environment, free-appropriate public education, due process procedures, and parent participation. The survey also elicited information regarding where school administrators received the majority of their knowledge about the six major principles (i.e., college coursework, district in-services, self-learning, on the job, or never learned).

Site and Population Characteristics

The state of Florida is comprised of 67 counties and each county has its own school district. In addition to the 67 county school districts, there are an additional seven districts that are composed of lab schools, juvenile detention center schools, virtual schools and specialty schools (e.g., deaf and blind). The population of this study was public school principals working at traditional public schools at the elementary, middle/junior high, and senior high schools across the state of Florida. Traditional public schools in Florida are defined as schools providing instruction at one or more grade levels from PK through Grade 12 (Florida Department of Education). Principals in charter schools, lab schools, combination schools (e.g., PK-8, 6-12, K-12), virtual schools, juvenile detention centers, and alternative/specialty schools were excluded from the total population. Due to the fact one of the 67 districts was entirely comprised of alternative/specialty schools, the number of school districts from which to draw principal participants decreased to 66. According to the Florida Department of Education's Master School Identification (MSID) file, as of June 21, 2011, within those 66 school districts there were 2,598 traditional public schools across the state of Florida. Of those schools, 1,701 were elementary schools, 513 were middle/junior high schools, and 384 were senior high schools.

Sampling Procedures

The researchers surveyed all traditional public school principals in the State of Florida. This sample size was determined to ensure the researchers would have enough respondents in order to generalize the findings. The schools were separated into elementary, middle/junior high, and senior high. The researchers obtained the principals' names and e-mails for the study by accessing the Florida Public Schools MSID file (Florida Department of Education, 2011). Once the information was retrieved from the file, the researchers then accessed each of the remaining 66 school district websites and located the name of each school's principal. If there was a discrepancy between the file and the district/school website, then the researchers obtained the correct contact and e-mail address from the district's/school's website or phoned the school for clarification. Once the list of names and e-mail addresses were finalized the number of principals to be surveyed was 2,598.

Instrumentation

Knowledge of special education policies and procedures was assessed using a two-part survey entitled, *Principals' Knowledge of Special Education Policies and Procedures* (PKSE) which was developed, piloted, and validated by the researchers. The first portion of the PKSE consisted of 18 questions that elicited school and principal demographics which later served as independent variables in the analysis of the data. The second portion of the PKSE consisted of 12 problem-based hypothetical scenarios concentrating on one or more of the six IDEA (2004) principles followed by four forced responses from which participants could choose. For each item, there was one correct response, two incorrect responses, and a fourth response participants could select if they were totally unfamiliar with the content. Following each survey item a secondary question was asked regarding the method by which school administrators purported to have learned the majority of their knowledge for that principle (i.e., college coursework, district in-services, self-learning on the job, or never learned this).

Instrument Validity and Usability

To ensure content validity of the instrument, the survey was reviewed and evaluated by six experts in the field of special education including a district level coordinator of exceptional student education, two school psychologists, and three program specialists in the Exceptional Student Education Department. Their input was used to revise questions and scenarios. Some revisions and minor changes were made to the wording of several of the forced responses and additional information was necessary for two of the twelve survey items (scenarios).

After content validity was reached, the survey was field tested for face validity in a doctoral level class with 22 students at a local university. Ease of understanding, readability, and instrument usability was tested through field administration of the survey with the director of exceptional student education in a nearby district. Necessary revisions were made in response to feedback to ensure survey reliability and to increase the validity of the subsequent findings of the study. A pilot study was also conducted and further helped to refine the instrumentation used in the study.

Finally, the survey was also piloted with five school principals who completed the survey electronically and in its entirety. Their resultant data was used to determine the reliability of the survey instrument. This was assessed using Cronbach's alpha. The Statistical Package for Social Sciences (SPSS) 19.0 was used to establish this estimate of internal consistency. It was determined that Cronbach's alpha reliability statistic for this instrument was .723. While Gay (1987) states that reliability coefficients greater than .9 are acceptable for any instrument, he cautions that lower coefficients are often acceptable with new instruments, at least initially. Further, George and Mallery (2003) expand on this by providing the commonly accepted rule of thumb for describing internal consistency, whereas alphas equal or greater than .7 are acceptable for judging the acceptability of the alpha.

Data Collection

The target population for this study was to consist of all traditional Florida public school principals across the 66 school districts. These districts accounted for 2,598 traditional (elementary, middle/junior high, and senior high) public schools.

However, after the initial cover letter, Internal Review Board (IRB) consent form, and survey were sent to the principals of the 2,598 traditional schools across 66 school districts, 9 separate school districts e-mailed the researchers indicating the district required its own approval process for any research to be conducted within the district. Despite the fact the researchers had secured IRB approval from Florida Atlantic University, nine of the 66 school districts denied the researchers access to survey the principals. Due to the time constraints of the study and the inordinate amount of extra work and time applying to nine separate school districts for research and IRB approval, the researchers elected to omit these school districts from the study and any participants from the nine school districts who responded were removed from the data. Therefore the sample decreased to 57 school districts and 1,493 schools/principals (973 elementary schools, 294 middle/junior high schools, and 226 senior high schools). However, an additional eight participants were invalidated for various reasons (such as email address was not valid, the principal was over multiple schools, etc.); therefore, the overall sample was 1,485 school principals (967 elementary schools, 292 middle/junior high schools, and 226 senior high schools). Of the 1,485 eligible principals, 176 participants completed the survey for a total response rate of 12%. Not included in the 12% response rate were 101 principals who only partially completed the survey, thus making their data incomplete and not comparable.

DATA ANALYSIS AND FINDINGS

The data collected through the survey was analyzed through the use of Statistical Package for the Social Sciences (SPSS) version 19.0 for Windows. Three statistical methods were employed to analyze the collected data. These included three Pearson product moment correlations, a t test, and seven ANOVAs. The outputs were used to respond to the research questions and test respective null hypotheses.

Descriptive Statistics

When analyzing the site demographics (see Table 4.1) of type of community ($N = 174$) and average daily attendance (ADA), it is worthy to note that the largest number of participants (89) led in suburban communities (51%) and 115 had an ADA of 500-999 students (65%). Additionally, 39 of

Table 4.1. Site Demographics

Type of Community (N=174)	N	Percentage (%)
Rural	39	23
Urban	46	26
Suburban	89	51
ADA		
Up to 499	26	15
500-999	115	65
1,000-1,499	18	10
1,500+	17	10

Table 4.2. Demographics of the Participants

	N	Percentage (%)
Grade Level	125	71
Elementary school	125	71
Middle school	28	16
High school	22	13
Gender		
Female	121	69
Male	55	31
Age		
25-34	2	1
35-44	36	20
45-54	66	38
55+	72	41
Years as a Principal		
1-5 years	75	43
6-10 years	55	31
11-15 years	26	15
16+ years	20	11

the principals led in rural communities (23%) and 46 of the principals led in urban communities (26%). A total of 26 principals had an ADA up to 499 students (15%), 18 principals had an ADA between 1000-1499 students (10%), and 17 principals had an ADA above 1,500 students (10%). It is interesting to note only the high schools responded as having above 1500 students and that number accounted for 77% of the high schools participating in the study.

An analysis of the demographics of the participants (see Table 4.2) showed that of the 176 returned surveys, 125 were elementary schools principals (71%); 28 were middle school principals (16%); and 22 were high school principals (13%). There were 121 females who participated in the study (69%) and 55 males who participated in the study (31%). Two of the participants were between the ages of 25-34 (1% of the sample tested). Thirty-six of the participants were between the ages of 35-44 (20% of the sample tested). Sixty-six of the participants were between the ages of 45-54 (38% of the sample tested). Seventy-two of the participants were age 55 or older, which accounted for the largest percentage of the sample (41% of the sample tested).

Finally, the largest percentage of the participants (43%) had only served as a school principal for 1-5 years. A total of 55 participants (31%) served as a school principal for 6-10 years, while 26 participants (15%) served as a school principal for 11-15 years. The remaining 20 participants (11%) served as a school principal for 16 or more years.

According to the survey responses inquiring about their backgrounds (see Table 4.3), 79 of the principals held a master's degree (45%), 45 held masters + 30 hours (26%), 20 held a specialist degree (11%), four had completed all of the coursework for a doctoral degree (2%), and 28 held a doctoral degree (16%). When asked if they had any prior teaching experience in the field of special education, 127 participants (72%) indicated they did not have any prior experience specifically teaching special education students, while 49 participants (28%) indicated they had experience teaching special education students. Of the 176 participants, 36

Table 4.3.   Background of Participants

	N	Percentage (%)
Highest Degree		
Master's	79	45
Master's + 30	45	26
Specialist	20	11
Doctorate	28	16
Other	4	2
Teaching Experience in Special Education		
No	127	72
Yes	49	28
Special Education Certified		
No	140	80
Yes	36	20

Table 4.4. Training and Education of Participants

	N	Percentage (%)
Courses in Special Education		
None	41	23
1-2	64	37
3-4	30	17
5+	41	23
Special Education Information Through Program		
Little–none	77	44
Some–substantial	99	56

(20%) were certified to teach in special education, while 140 (80%) held no special education certification.

When asked about coursework and training in special education (see Table 4.4), 41 participants (23%) indicated they did not take any formal coursework in special education at the college/university level. The highest number, 64 participants (37%), indicated they took one to two courses at the college/university in special education. A total of 30 participants (17%) indicated they took three to four courses at the college/university in special education and 41 participants (23%) indicated they took five or more courses in special education at the college/university level. Further, the participants were asked "How much information about special education programs/laws do you feel you received in your education administration/leadership licensing or degree (master's, specialist, PhD, EdD) program?"

The results were interesting in that 44% of the participants indicated they received little to no information regarding special education programs/laws during their education administration/leadership licensing or degree programs.

For the purposes of this study, the researchers also sought to determine the amount of participation in special education in-services provided through the participants' respective school districts and also participation in in-services, conferences, and workshops (see Table 4.5). When asked, "Approximately how many formal special education in-services (provided through your school district) have you participated in over the past 2 years?" 12 participants (7%) responded they did not participate in any special education in-services. Most participants (46%) participated in one to two special education in-services over the past 2 years. A total of 44 participants (25%) participated in three to four in-services over the past 2

Table 4.5. In-Service, Workshop, and Conference Training of Respondents

	N	Percentage (%)
District Special Education In-Services		
None	12	7
1-2	81	46
3-4	44	25
5+	39	22
Special Education In-Services, Workshops, and Conferences (N = 173)		
Never	31	18
Yearly	102	59
Quarterly	30	17
Monthly	10	6

Table 4.6. Form of Greatest Assistance for Special Education Needs of Respondents

Form of Assistance	Total Score[1]	Overall Rank
Coordinator/consultant	871	1
District/central office	797	2
Special Ed. teacher	772	3
Policy manuals	712	4
Professional literature	645	5
Conferences/workshops	638	6
Assistant principal	458	7
Special Ed. coursework	368	8

Note: 1. Score is a weighted calculation. Items ranked first are valued higher than the following ranks; the score is the sum of all weighted rank counts.

years, while 39 participants (22%) participated in five or more in-services over the past 2 years. Finally, the participants were asked, "How frequently do you attend special education in-services, conferences, or workshops?" The results showed 31 participants (18%) never attend special education in-services, conferences, or workshops; 102 participants (59%) attend special education in-services, conferences, or workshops annually; 30 participants (17%) attend special education in-services, conferences, or workshops four times a year; and 10 participants (6%) attend special education in-services, conferences, or workshops monthly.

Finally, the participants were asked to rank from most to least (1 = *most* and 8 = *least*) where they felt they received the majority of their assistance and support in terms of their professional needs with regards to special education (see Table 4.6). The scores were a weighted calculation. Items ranked first were valued higher than the following ranks. Items ranked as number ones were given a score value of eight, and each subsequent number was given a diminished value (7, 6, 5 …). The total score is the sum of all weighted rank counts; therefore the highest total score was given the overall rank of one, while the lowest total score was given the overall rank of eight. Findings indicated the participants received the most assistance and support from the special education coordinator/consultant (school based), followed by the central office, special education teacher, policy manuals, professional literature, conferences and workshops, the assistant principal, and finally the least amount of assistance through special education coursework at a college/university.

PRINCIPALS' KNOWLEDGE OF SPECIAL EDUCATION POLICIES AND PROCEDURES

One of the overarching research questions in this study was: What knowledge do Florida principals possess in the area of special education policies and procedures, as defined by the Individuals with Disabilities Education Improvement Act of 2004? To assist in the investigation of this question, an item analysis and summary of the responses to the hypothetical scenarios, grouped by the six principles of IDEA 2004: zero reject, nondiscriminatory evaluation, least restrictive environment, free-appropriate public education, due process, and parent participation (see Table 4.7) will be described. Following this summary, a second item analysis will be presented for the following overarching research question (see Table 4.8): What was the primary method (i.e., college coursework, district in-services, self learning, on the job, or did not learn this) by which principals purport to have learned the majority of special education policies and procedures?

The six principles of special education policies and procedures, as defined under IDEA 2004, were tested and demonstrated an overall mean score of 5.74, which equates to 48%. Participants' scores ranged from 8% correct to 100% correct. However, only 20 participants received an overall score of 75% or higher. Of these 20 participants, there did not appear to be any specific characteristics that they all shared, which would account for their higher score on the PKSE.

Major areas of concern were those items in which the participants had a higher percentage of responses with the incorrect answer than the correct answer. Each of the six areas had one out of the two questions with a greater percentage of participants answering incorrectly. For the principle

Table 4.7.   Item Analysis Results for Hypothetical Scenarios

Item (N)	Area	A	B	C	Don't Know	Correct Answer	Percent Correct
20 (171)	Zero reject	23	68	61	19	B	40
21 (171)	Zero reject	3	57	104	7	C	61
23 (172)	Evaluation	155	6	8	3	A	90
24 (171)	Evaluation	63	59	32	17	C	19
26 (170)	LRE	23	94	18	35	B	55
27 (169)	LRE	83	19	12	55	A	49
29 (166)	FAPE	47	6	45	68	A	28
30 (164)	FAPE	7	20	90	47	C	55
32 (165)	Due process	9	94	43	19	B	57
33(163)	Due process	51	34	40	38	C	25
35 (163)	Parents	6	56	57	44	C	35
36 (165)	Parents	118	22	10	15	A	72

Table 4.8.   Item Analysis Results of Where Principals Report to Have Received Knowledge

Item (N)	Area	College Courses	District In-Services	Self Taught	On the Job	Did Not Learn
22 (173)	Zero reject	3%	22%	4%	26%	45%
25 (170)	Evaluation	5%	35%	4%	40%	16%
28 (171)	LRE	13%	41%	3%	34%	9%
31 (168)	FAPE	13%	35%	5%	33%	14%
24 (166)	Due process	5%	34%	4%	46%	11%
37 (166)	Parents	4%	45%	3%	39%	9%

of zero reject (Item 20), 60% of participants incorrectly answered the hypothetical scenario dealing with prior knowledge of a suspected disability. Additionally, 81% of participants incorrectly answered the hypothetical scenario dealing with parental consent for initial placement under the principle of nondiscriminatory evaluation (Item 24). Under the principle of least restrictive environment (Item 26), 51% incorrectly answered the scenario dealing with a student's classroom placement. Likewise, 72% of the participants incorrectly answered the scenario dealing with a student who received a special diploma but wanted to return to school the following fall, under the principle of free-appropriate public education (Item 29). Under the principle of due process (Item 33), 75% of the participants incorrectly answered the scenario dealing with the "stay-put" clause and placement in alternative educational settings during due process proceedings. Finally, 65% of participants incorrectly answered the scenario dealing with parental revocation of consent for special education and related services, under the parent participation principle (Item 35).

Where Principals Acquired Their Knowledge of Special Eduation Policies and Procedures

The principals were then asked the primary method by which they learned the majority of special education policies and procedures for each of the six principles of IDEA 2004 (see Table 4.8). The table portrays the six principles of IDEA 2004 and the percentage of principals who report learning the knowledge for each through the following methods: college coursework, district in-services, self-taught, on the job, as well as the percentage of principals who reported not to have learned this knowledge. It is important to note the majority of the participants felt they received the most knowledge about the particular topic in five of the six areas from either district in-services or learning while on the job. The one exception to this is in the area of zero reject, where 45% of participants claimed to have never learned this information.

STATISTICAL ANALYSES

This section includes the corresponding statistical data analyses for each of the research questions. Through the use of Statistical Package for the Social Sciences (SPSS) version 19.0 for Windows, three statistical methods were employed to analyze the collected data. These analyses included a t test, three Pearson product moment correlations, and seven ANOVAs. The outputs were used to respond to the research subquestions and test their respective null hypotheses.

Formal Training

The first research subquestion investigated whether or not principals who receive formal training (i.e., any level of college coursework in any program area) in special education have a greater level of overall knowledge in the area of special education policies and procedures than principals who did not receive formal training in special education? The null hypothesis for this question indicated there is no significant difference in the level of overall knowledge in the area of special education policies and procedures between principals who received formal training in special education and those who did not receive formal training in special education.

A Pearson product moment correlation was conducted using the following variables: the knowledge score (level of knowledge of special education policies and procedures) and formal training (number of courses). The alpha level was set at .05 to determine if any relationship existed between the knowledge score and the formal training in special education. The results show a positive correlation between receiving formal special education training and a participant's knowledge of special education policies and procedures, which was found to be statistically significant ($r = .202$, $n = 171$, $p < .05$). As a result of this small effect size ($r = .202$), the correlation result, while statistically significant, is not considered to be of much practical significance. An ANOVA (see Table 4.9) was then used to test for the difference between the four means and determine whether there were any significant differences between the means of the knowledge scores and the amount of formal training in special education (i.e., number of special education classes taken).

Levene's test of homogeneity of variance, which tests for similar variances, was found not to be significant ($p = .476$). Consequently, the assumption of homogeneity of variance was met. Results from the one-way ANOVA for this hypothesis indicate among Florida principals responding to the survey ($N = 171$) there were statistically significant differences between the means of the knowledge scores and the amount of formal training in special education (i.e., number of special education classes taken) $F(3, 167) = 3.253$, $p < 0.05$. Therefore, the null hypothesis that there is no significant difference in overall knowledge of special education policies and procedures between principals who received formal training and those who did not receive formal training was rejected.

Table 4.9. ANOVA for Principals' Knowledge of Special Education Policies and Procedures by Number of Special Education Courses Taken

	Sum of Squares	df	Mean Square	F	P
Between groups	45.314	3	15.105	3.253	.023
Within groups	775.364	167	4.643		
Total	820.678	170			

Further, a Tukey post-hoc test was run. It revealed that the knowledge of special education policies and procedures was statistically significantly higher after taking five or more special education courses. Based on the eta value for effect size, it is determined the effect size is just below that of a medium effect (χ^2 = .055, where .06 is considered a medium effect), and thus is considered relatively small and not considered to be of much practical significance.

Method of Learning

The second research subquestion investigated the relationship between the principals' knowledge levels in the area of special education policies and procedures, as defined by the six principles of IDEA 2004, and the method by which they received the majority of their knowledge for each area. The null hypothesis for this question indicated there is no significant relationship between principals' knowledge levels in the area of special education policies and procedures, as defined by the six principles of IDEA 2004, and the methods by which they received the majority of their knowledge for each area.

The null hypothesis was tested for a statistically significant difference in principals' knowledge of special education policies and procedures, as defined by the six areas of IDEA 2004, against the method by which they received the majority of their knowledge for each area. Six, one-way ANOVAs were performed (see Table 4.10). The ANOVAs showed no significant difference between principals' knowledge of special education policies and procedures, in the six principles of IDEA 2004, and the method of knowledge acquisition. Therefore, null hypothesis two that there is no significant relationship between principals' knowledge levels in special education, as defined by the six areas of IDEA 2004, and the methods by which they received the majority of their knowledge for each area failed to be rejected.

Prior Teaching Experience

The third research subquestion investigated whether principals who have prior teaching experience in the field of special education have a greater level of overall knowledge in the area of special education policies and procedures than principals who do not have prior teaching experience in the field of special education. The null hypothesis for this question indicated there is no significant difference in the level of overall knowledge in the area of special education policies and procedures

**Table 4.10. ANOVA for Principals' Knowledge
of Special Education Policies and Procedures, as Defined
by the Six Areas of IDEA 2004, by Method of Knowledge Acquisition**

	Sum of Squares	Df	Mean Square	F	P
Zero Reject Total					
Between groups	.608	3	.203	.385	.764
Within groups	47.392	90	.527		
Total	48.000	93			
Evaluation Total					
Between groups	.729	3	.234	.974	.407
Within groups	34.454	138	.250		
Total	35.183	141			
LRE Total					
Between groups	.189	3	.063	.098	.961
Within groups	96.149	150	.641		
Total	96.338	153			
FAPE Total					
Between groups	.106	3	.035	.075	.973
Within groups	64.880	138	.470		
Total	64.986	141			
Due Process Total					
Between groups	1.157	3	.386	1.078	.361
Within groups	50.066	140	.358		
Total	51.222	143			
Parent Participation Total					
Between groups	.763	3	.254	.519	.670
Within groups	70.534	144	.490		
Total	71.297	147			

between principals who have prior teaching experience in the field of special education and those who do not have prior teaching experience in the field of special education.

According to Table 4.4, 72% of the Florida principals surveyed (127 participants) had no prior teaching experience in the field of special education, where 28% of the Florida principals surveyed (49 participants) had prior teaching experience in the field of special education. A t test was conducted to compare the means between the principals' overall knowledge of special education policies and procedures and past teaching experience in the field of special education. The assumption of homogeneity of variance was tested by Levene's test for equality of variances and the p value was greater than .05 ($p = .719$), thus confirming the assumption of equal variance. This study found there was a statistically significant difference between the two groups, Group 1: Yes Teaching Experience ($M = 6.43$, $SD = 2.030$) and Group 2: No Teaching Experience ($M = 5.48$, $SD = 2.210$), $t(169) = 2.542$, $p < .05$. Therefore, the null hypothesis that there is no significant relationship between the principals' overall knowledge in the area of special education policies and procedures and past teaching experience in the field of special education was rejected. Further, using a pooled estimate of the standard deviation: Cohen's $d = 6.43 - 5.48/ \sqrt{((2.030^2 + 2.210^2)/2)}$. Therefore, Cohen's effect size value ($d = .4477$) suggested a medium practical significance.

School Size and Community Type

The fourth research subquestion investigated whether the level of overall knowledge in the area of special education policies and procedures is similar among principals across different school sizes, as measured by school enrollment. The null hypothesis for this question indicated there is no significant difference in the level of overall knowledge in the area of special education policies and procedures among principals across different school sizes, as measured by school enrollment.

A Pearson product-moment correlation was run to determine the relationship between a participant's overall knowledge in the area of special education policies and procedures and school enrollment, $r(171) = 0.080$, $p > 0.05$. The results were not statistically significant ($p = .297$). Therefore, null hypothesis four that there is no significant relationship in the overall knowledge in the area of special education policies and procedures between principals across different school sizes failed to be rejected.

Finally, the fifth research subquestion investigated whether the level of overall knowledge in the area of special education policies and procedures is similar among principals across community types (i.e., rural, suburban, and urban). The null hypothesis for this question indicated there is no significant difference in the level of overall knowledge in the area of special education policies and procedures among principals across community types.

The three types of communities: rural, suburban, and urban, were coded ordinally as one, two, and three, respectively. A Pearson product-moment correlation was run to determine the relationship between a participant's overall knowledge in the area of special education policies and procedures and the type of community in which their school is located, $r(169) = 0.016, p > 0.05$. The results were not statistically significant ($p = .840$). Therefore, null hypothesis five that there is no significant difference in the overall knowledge in the area of special education policies and procedures among principals across rural, suburban, and urban schools in the state of Florida failed to be rejected.

DISCUSSION OF FINDINGS

The overarching research questions explored (a) the level of knowledge Florida principals possess in the area of special education policies and procedures, as defined by IDEA 2004, and (b) the primary method by which principals purport to have learned the majority of special education policies and procedures for each of the six principles of IDEA 2004. The following sections of the chapter discuss the study's overall findings as well as the two statistically significant ancillary findings, with specific regard to existing literature and in light of the conceptual framework used to guide the study's design and analysis. The conclusions section will attempt to understand the study's findings by applying the study's conceptual frames, social justice and ethical reasoning in educational leadership, to the findings broadly to better recognize how principals' knowledge in the area of special education policies and procedures interacts with social justice and ethical reasoning in education policy.

Knowledge of Special Education Policies and Procedures

The six principles of special education policies and procedures, as defined under IDEA 2004, were tested and demonstrated an overall mean score of 5.74, which equates to 48%. Therefore, of the 176 school leaders whose knowledge of special education policies and procedures were assessed, the average score was 48%. Consequently, the findings of this study suggest that most of the school leaders in Florida who participated in the research responded incorrectly to more than half of the questions on the survey designed to assess their knowledge of special education policies and procedures. In most cases, a 48% correct response rate on any assessment is considered failing. Therefore, the finding is suggestive that school principals in Florida do not hold a sufficient amount of knowledge in the area of special education policies and procedures.

Specifically, when broken down by area, it was determined the mean knowledge scores of principals regarding each of the six principles of

IDEA 2004 were considerably low. The percentage of correct responses for each of the six principles were as follows: zero reject policy had a 50% correct response rate; the nondiscriminatory evaluation policy had a 55% correct response rate; the least restrictive environment policy had a 52% correct response rate; the free-appropriate public education policy had a 41% correct response rate; the due process policy had a 40% correct response rate; and the parent participation policy had a 53% correct response rate. This data suggests principal knowledge to be the weakest in the areas of free-appropriate public education and due process.

These findings are synonymous with the results of previous studies in the field, which indicated a lack of educational training and preparation in the area of special education for school leaders (Aspedon, 1992; Dickenson et al., 2003). Similarly, McClard-Bertrand and Bratberg (2007) found more extensive formal training in the special education field is essential if school leaders are to have the knowledge necessary to operate successful special education programs in their schools. These findings also support the prior research of DiPaola and Walther-Thomas (2003) who found "most principals lack the course work and field experience needed to lead local efforts to create learning environments that emphasize academic success for students with disabilities" (p. 11). Gaps in training regarding special education policies and procedures as reported by Rhys (1996) and Nardone (1999) confirm the lack of preparation by stating school principals are deficient in their knowledge of special education legal issues. Further, findings from this study reflect extensive research (Davidson & Algozzine, 2002; Valesky & Hirth, 1992; Wakeman, Browder, Meier, & McColl, 2007) that reveals dissonance between what education leadership preparation programs are providing future school leaders and the knowledge they will need for the demands of the job.

This lack of knowledge suggests there may be some concerns in the areas of social justice and ethical reasoning as they relate to special education. "Most importantly, principals' lack of knowledge of these regulations may affect the outcome of services for students with disabilities" (Cooner, Tochterman, & Garrison-Wade, 2004, n.p.). If this is indeed true, the students, programs, and special education teachers will suffer.

Methods of Knowledge Acquisition

The principals were then asked the primary method by which they acquired the majority of their knowledge of special education policies and procedures for each of the six principles of IDEA 2004. The overall mean percentages showed 7% of the principals acquired the majority of their knowledge through college coursework; another 35.3% of the principals

**Table 4.11.   Methods By Which
Principals Report To Have Received Knowledge**

IDEA 2004 Principle	College Courses	District In-Services	Self Taught	On the Job	Did Not Learn
Zero reject	3%	22%	4%	26%	45%
Evaluation	5%	35%	4%	40%	16%
LRE	13%	41%	3%	34%	9%
FAPE	13%	35%	5%	33%	14%
Due process	5%	34%	4%	46%	11%
Parents	4%	45%	3%	39%	9%

acquired the majority of their knowledge through district in-services; 4% of the principals acquired the majority of their knowledge through the method of self teaching; 36.3% of the principals acquired the majority of their knowledge through the method of on the job experiences; and 17.3% of the principals claimed never to have learned this information.

When the methods of knowledge acquisitions were separated according to the six principles of IDEA 2004 (see Table 4.11), the percentage of principals who acquired their knowledge through college courses, district in-services, self-taught, on the job, and those who did not learn the information were as follows for each principle. The zero reject principle percentages were: 3%, 22%, 4%, 26%, and 45%, respectively. The nondiscriminatory evaluation principle percentages were: 5%, 35%, 4%, 40%, and 16%, respectively. The least restrictive environment principle percentages were: 13%, 41%, 3%, 34%, and 9%, respectively. The free-appropriate public education principle percentages were: 13%, 35%, 5%, 33%, and 14%, respectively. The due process principle percentages were: 5%, 34%, 4%, 46%, and 11%, respectively. Finally, the parent participation principle percentages were: 4%, 45%, 3%, 39%, and 9%, respectively.

An analysis of the methods by which principals purport to have acquired their overall knowledge in the area of special education policies and procedures across all six principles suggests that the majority of participants acquired the knowledge through district in-services and on the job experiences. This finding suggests principal preparation programs may be inadequate in providing the necessary knowledge of special education policies and procedures. This supports the prior research of Hess and Kelly (2005) who concluded, "Because preparation of principals has not kept pace with changes in the larger world of schooling, graduates of principal preparation programs have been left ill equipped for the challenges and opportunities posed by an era of accountability" (p. 40). Capper et al. (2006) call for increased attention to assessing preparation programs and how they prepare school leaders for social justice. Further, Laskey and Karge (2006) surveyed 205 principals in California and found that although the majority of principals considered formal training in special education as very important, many indicated little to no direct experience working with students with disabilities in their preparation programs. Similarly, Wakeman et al. (2007) reported that principals had "received little (47.8%) or some (37.6%) information about special education in their principal licensing program" (p. 158). Little or some information has not proven adequate in providing the necessary knowledge of special education policies and procedures. Finally, Lust (2005) reported that 77.6% of principals indicated principal preparation programs did not prepare them to deal with the special education issues they faced once on the job. All of these findings indicate a dearth of included knowledge in the area of special education policies and procedures in most school leadership programs.

This overall finding is consistent with the data for each individual principle of IDEA 2004, with the exception of the zero reject principle where 45% of the principals claimed never to have learned the information. Thus, having been unable to report where or even if they had received knowledge of the zero reject principle, this finding suggests a gap in training across colleges and school districts. This is consistent with earlier findings of similar studies that indicated a lack of special education training for school leaders (Aspedon, 1992; Dickenson et al., 2003; McClard-Bertrand & Bratberg, 2007).

Amount of Coursework

Further findings from this study revealed the knowledge of special education policies and procedures was statistically significantly higher after taking five or more special education courses. This finding suggests broad training in special education is needed if school leaders are to have knowledge of special education policies and procedures. This finding aligns with the research of McClard-Bertrand and Bratberg (2007), who concluded more extensive formal training in the special education field is necessary if school leaders are to have the knowledge necessary to operate successful special education programs in their schools. Further, it supports the findings of Patterson et al. (2000), who found administrators who obtained special training or professional development related to educating students with disabilities indicated such training and background as beneficial to their leadership role in special education at the school level.

Career Path

The final finding indicated that principals who had prior teaching experience in the field of special education had a greater overall knowledge in the area of special education policies and procedures than those who did not have prior teaching experience in the field of special education. However, it is unknown if this finding potentially has a confounding influence; perhaps the participants who taught in special education also received formal education in the field of special education. However, this finding still suggests that actually having personal experience with students with disabilities can increase one's knowledge of the policies and procedures in the field of special education.

This aligns with the previous research regarding personal experiences with people with disabilities. Praisner (2003) and Wakeman (2005) found that having personal experience with people with disabilities had a clear relationship with the principal's attitude and fundamental knowledge of special education. However, other prior research in the field looked at an increase in special education knowledge in relation to teaching experience in general, not specific to teaching in the field of special education. Therefore, this study's comparison of the knowledge in the area of special education between those principals who had teaching experience in special education and those who did not have teaching experience in special education is a contribution to the literature. Nevertheless, the following studies did look at principals' knowledge level and years of experience as a teacher in general. Hirth (1988) found that principals' knowledge of special education was related with their years of experience as a teacher and Claxton (2002) found principals' knowledge levels in special education were positively correlated to their years of teaching experience. On the other hand, Copenhaver (2005) and Power (2007) each found that there was no significant difference in principal knowledge when compared to teaching experience.

CONCLUSIONS

In examining the four significant findings, it is logical to conclude there is an absolute gap in principal training when it comes to their readiness to lead schools that enroll students with disabilities, which happens to be most, if not all, public schools. While there are areas where some principals, although most often the minority of study participants, demonstrated a greater degree of knowledge of special education policies and procedures, in no way do their scores suggest any level of expertise. As mentioned in the previous section, this fact alone is disconcerting and absolutely begs that principal training programs be reexamined for gaps in these particular areas of knowledge. However, and perhaps even more disconcerting, is how ignorance of special education policies and procedures correlates with injustice across special education policy.

Social justice as defined by Adams et al. (1997) and ethical reasoning in educational leadership developed and defined by Shapiro and Stefkovich (2005) were chosen as the conceptual framework with which to guide the design and analysis of the study. In looking at principal preparation in regards to special education through a combination of conceptual lenses and paradigms, the researchers hoped to identify the levels of equity among the opportunities provided for children with special needs.

The following sections discuss the findings of the study using the conceptual frames of social justice and ethical reasoning in educational leadership discussed earlier. Using these lenses, several implications arise for current principals and principal preparation programs. By utilizing these frameworks, one can assess if enough training is provided to school principals in the area of special education policies and procedures, to ensure they are equipped to provide equitable and socially just educational opportunities for students with disabilities in the public school systems.

Social Justice

Foster (1986) expressed the ideology of ethics best when he wrote: "Each administrative decision carries with it a restructuring of human life: that is why administration at its heart is the resolution of moral dilemmas" (p. 33). Unless school leaders are trained in the area of moral reasoning and, more specifically, social justice, the inequities we see today will most likely remain. Greenfield (1993) stressed the importance for such training in moral reasoning when he stated:

> A failure to provide the opportunity for school administrators to develop such competence constitutes a failure to serve children we are obligated to serve as public educators. As a profession, educational administration thus has a moral obligation to train prospective administrators to be able to apply the principles, rules, ideals, and virtues associated with the development of ethical schools. (p. 285)

In considering the findings that school principals in Florida may not hold a sufficient amount of knowledge in the area of special education policies and procedures, it is suggested not enough training in special education exists in our principal preparation programs. These individuals are expected to be the instructional leaders in their schools, yet they do not have the fundamental knowledge necessary to ensure the rights given to a percentage of their total school population are not being violated. In fact, they do not have sufficient knowledge to ensure they, themselves, are not violating these particular rights. What good are rights, if those who hold the power are oblivious to them? What good are laws, when they do not stretch far enough, and those who are left to interpret them may possibly lack the knowledge and moral reasoning needed to guarantee the laws are followed with the intent in which they were written?

Another finding from this research indicated the methods by which principals purport to have learned the majority of their knowledge of special education policies and procedures, across the six principles of IDEA 2004, may not be effective in providing sufficient or accurate knowledge. Principals claimed to have received the majority of their knowledge either from district in-services or on the job for the principles of nondiscriminatory evaluation, least restrictive environment, free-appropriate public education, due process, and parental participation. With the overall low test scores in this study, the level of district training should be questioned. Further, those individuals who felt they learned the majority of their knowledge on the job should reevaluate how this knowledge was learned. If they are asking other individuals to assume special education responsibilities or receiving their information from other individuals, these individuals may be just as unprepared and unknowledgeable in the area of special education policies and procedures as the principal (Smith & Colon, 1998). Without this direct knowledge of special education policies and procedures, principals simply cannot provide equitable and socially just educational opportunities to students with disabilities.

Ethical Reasoning in Educational Leadership

In the following framework, "four approaches to ethical analysis are presented that influence the practice of school leaders, including the perspectives of justice, critique, care, and the ethics of one's profession" (Lashley, 2007, p. 182). These four approaches are interwoven, and when used together, this paradigm model can assist in solving moral dilemmas. Following is a brief description of each approach in the paradigm model and how it applies to the findings of this study.

Ethic of justice

The ethic of justice focuses on rights and laws. It looks to see if there is a law, right, or policy that relates to a particular case. For the purpose of this research we will use the Individuals with Disabilities Education Improvement Act of 2004. A school principal has to be aware of the "rights inherent in IDEA and why they are in place.... He or she must also know the legal and policy requirements of the law, as well as understand the historical and educational contexts that have led to these requirements" (Lashley, 2007, p. 184).

Examining the findings of this study through the ethic of justice, it is suggested school principals do not have the basic knowledge of IDEA 2004 or the necessary knowledge of the legal and policy requirements of the law. An overall score of 48% in the knowledge of special education policies and procedures, as assessed by the PKSE, suggests a lack of knowledge of the policies and procedures across the six principles of IDEA 2004. It is the recommendation of the researchers that a policy be put in place to require specific special education training on IDEA 2004 within principal preparation programs.

Ethic of Critique

The ethic of critique is based on critical theory, which has, at its heart, an analysis of social class and its inequities. Giroux (1991) asserts the ethic of critique provides "a discourse for expanding basic human rights" (p. 48). It is "aimed at awakening educators to inequities in society and, in particular, in the schools" (Shapiro & Stefkovich, 2005, p. 16). The ethic of critique raises hard questions concerning the treatment of diverse groups in society: issues of oppression, domination, and discrimination can be taken into account (Shapiro & Stefkovich, 2005). In the ethic of critique, questions are asked such as: "who benefits from the law, rule, or policy...who are the silenced voices?" (Shapiro & Stefkovich, 2005, p. 16).

Examining the findings of this study through the ethic of critique, it is clear the silenced voices belong to the students with disabilities. With school leaders lacking the knowledge to ensure they are following the law and leading in the best interest of students with disabilities, school leaders could in fact be continuing to oppress and silence this group. If the school leader cannot stand up for the rights of students with disabilities because they lack the knowledge to do so, who will become the voice for these students? The ethic of critique portrays the need for a policy to be put in place requiring specific special education training on IDEA 2004 within the principal preparation programs.

Ethic of Care

According to I. Young (1990), to achieve equity "social policy should sometimes afford special treatment to groups" (p. 158). This concept provides a case for unequal treatment for those who have been disadvantaged over time. Aristotle "held that justice consists in treating equals equally and unequals unequally" (Strike & Soltis, 1992, p. 46).

The ethic of care places equity at the center of the paradigm. Using this paradigm, the voices of the diverse groups, particularly those who have been discriminated against, are heard (I. Young, 1990). This paradigm asks basic questions such as who will benefit from what I decide; who will be hurt by the decisions; and what are the long term effects of the decision I make today?

Considering the findings of this study through the ethic of care, it is suggested the mere neglect of knowledge required of school leaders causes one to wonder what the long term effect of the absence of standards might be and how this would impact students with disabilities. The effects are portentous; it is difficult to imagine such a lack of knowledge in respect to special education policies and procedures would not ultimately result in creating inequitable opportunities for students with disabilities. Again, the need for a policy to be put in place to require specific special education training on IDEA 2004 within the principal preparation programs is evident under the ethic of care.

Ethic of the Profession

Using the ethic of the profession, we understand that how our schools address the evolving needs of our students, who are diverse in nature, will determine the success of our schools and our nation (Shapiro & Stefkovich, 2005). "In educational administration, we believe that if there is a moral imperative for the profession, it is to serve the best interests of the student [including those with disabilities]" (Shapiro & Stefkovich, 2005, p. 26). Looking at the findings of the research through this lens, it suggests principal preparation programs and school districts may not be providing the level of intensity and types of supports needed for school leaders to serve the best interest of students with disabilities. The overall lack of knowledge in this area hinders school leaders from even knowing what is in the best interest of their students with disabilities. In knowing the current policy, which dictates Florida Principal Leadership Standards, is not based on the best interests of students with disabilities, it would not be professionally ethical to follow these standards.

IMPLICATIONS

This study suggests that principals' knowledge of special education policies and procedures does indeed matter if there is an assumption of social justice underpinning educational leadership preparation. While principals are expected to be the instructional leaders in their schools, they may not have the fundamental knowledge necessary to ensure the rights, given to a percentage of their school population, are not being violated.

Examining the findings of this research through the dual lenses of social justice and ethical reasoning, it can be suggested that there is a lack of training being provided to school principals in the area of special education policies and procedures. If society is interested in ensuring principals are equipped to provide equitable and socially just educational opportunities for students with disabilities, appropriate training must be provided. There is a strong need for a policy to be put in place to require specific special education training on IDEA 2004 within the principal preparation programs. Lashley (2007) expressed the current need when he stated:

> A new understanding of the school leader's accountability for the education of all students—an understanding that emerges from the knowledge traditions of special and general education, the provisions of the IDEA and No Child Left Behind Act, and the wisdom of practice—is necessary to focus on leadership, not only for school improvement, but for social justice, equity, and democracy in schools. (p. 186)

With accountability and evaluations being tied to student performance, as measured by high-stakes standardized testing, insurmountable issues have arisen in regards to evaluating teaching and subsequently leading the education of students with disabilities. When principals lack the necessary knowledge of special education policies and procedures, yet are required to evaluate special education teachers and programs, the teachers, programs, and subsequently the students with disabilities are set up for inevitable failure. It is like trying to fly a plane while still putting together the pieces. It will not end well.

REFERENCES

Adams, M., Bell, L. A., & Griffin, P. (1997). *Teaching for diversity and social justice* (2nd ed.). New York, NY: Routledge.

Aronson, J. (2004). The threat of stereotype. *Educational Leadership, 62*(3), 14-19.

Aspedon, M. (1992, April). *Principals' attitudes toward special education: Results and implications on a comprehensive research study.* Paper presented at the Council for Exceptional Children 70th Annual Convention, Baltimore, MD.

Boeckmann, M. E., & Dickinson, G. B. (2001). Leadership: Values and performance. *Education, 121*(3), 494-497.

Bogotch, I. (2002a). Educational leadership and social justice: Practice into theory. *Journal of School Leadership, 12*(2), 138-156.

Bogotch, I. (2002b). "Enmeshed in the work": The educative power of developing standards. *Journal of School Leadership, 12*(5), 503-525.

Capper, C. A., Theoharis, G., & Sebastian, J. (2006). Toward a framework for preparing leaders for social justice. *Journal of Educational Administration, 44*(3), 209-224.

Claxton, C. W. (2002). *The relationship between principals' knowledge of disability laws and their disciplinary practices in Georgia elementary schools* (Doctoral dissertation). Available from ProQuest Dissertations and Theses database. (UMI No. 3041643)

Cooner, D., Tochterman, S., & Garrison-Wade, D. (2004). Preparing principals for leadership in special education: Applying ISLLC standards. *Connections: Journal of Principal Preparation and Development, 6,* 19-24.

Copenhaver, M. B. (2005). *Survey of North Carolina principals' knowledge of special education law* (Doctoral dissertation). Available from ProQuest Dissertations and Theses database. (UMI No. 3185748)

The Council of Chief State School Officers. (2008). *Education leadership policy standards: ISLLC 2008.* Washington, DC: Author.

Creighton, T. (2002). Standards for education administration preparation programs: Okay, but don't we have the cart before the horse? *Journal of School Leadership, 12*(5), 526-551.

Crockett, J. B. (2002). Special education's role in preparing responsive leaders for inclusive schools. *Remedial and Special Education, 23*(3), 157-68.

Davidson, D. N., & Algozzine, B. (2002). Administrators' perceptions of special education law. *Journal of Special Education Leadership, 15*(2), 43-48.

Dickenson, W., Knopp, T., & Fauske, J. (2003). *Special education practice and policy: What principals know and need to know.* Unpublished manuscript, College of Education, University of South Florida at Tampa.

DiPaola, M. F., & Tschannen-Moran, M. (2003). The principalship at a crossroads: A study of the conditions and concerns of principals. *National Association of Secondary School Principals, 87*(634), 43-65.

DiPaola, M. F., & Walther-Thomas, C. (2003). *Principals and special education: The critical role of school leaders* (COPPSE Document No. 1B-7). Gainesville, FL: University of Florida, Center on Personnel Studies in Special Education.

Doyle, L. H. (2001, April). *Leadership and inclusion: Reculturing for reform.* Paper presented at the Annual meeting of the American Educational Research Association, Seattle, WA.

Duncan, A. (2010, November). *Fulfilling the promise of IDEA.* Speech presented at the 35th Anniversary of the Individuals with Disabilities Education Act, Washington, DC.

English, F. W. (2001, April). *The epistemological foundations of professional practice: Do they matter? The case for the ISLLC Standards and the National Exam for Administrative Licensure.* Paper presented at the annual meeting of the American Educational Research Association, Seattle, WA.

Florida Department of Education (FLDOE). (2005). *Florida school leaders: The Florida principal leadership standards.* Retrieved from https://www.floridaschoolleaders.org/fpls.aspx

Florida Department of Education. (2006). *Florida school leaders: The William Cecil Golden School Leadership Development Program.* Retrieved from https://www.floridaschoolleaders.org/delta-overview.aspx

Florida Department of Education. (2011). *Master identification file 2011-2012*. Retrieved from http://doewebprd.doe.state.fl.us/EDS/MasterSchoolID/

Florida State Board of Education. (2007). *Approval of school leadership programs*. Retrieved from https://www.flrules.org/gateway/readFile.asp?sid= 0&tid=4253855&type=1&File= 6A-5.081.doc

Foster, W. (1986). *Paradigms and promises: New approaches to educational administration*. Buffalo, NY: Prometheus Books.

Foster, W. (2003, April). *National standards and local curriculum*. Paper presented at the annual meeting of the American Educational Research Association, Chicago, IL.

Gay, L. R. (1987). *Educational research: Competencies for analysis and application* (3rd ed.). New York, NY: Macmillan.

George, D., & Mallery, P. (2003). *SPSS for Windows step by step: A simple guide and reference*. 11.0 update (4th ed.). Boston, MA: Allyn & Bacon.

Giroux, H. A. (1991). *Postmodernism, feminism, and cultural politics: Redrawing educational boundaries*. Albany, NY: State University of New York Press.

Green, R. L. (2001). *Practicing the art of leadership: A problem-based approach to implementing the ISLLS standards*. Columbus, OH: Merrill Prentice Hall.

Greenfield, W. D. (1993). Articulating values and ethics in administrator preparation. In C. Capper (Ed.), *Educational administration in a pluralistic society* (pp. 267- 287). Albany, NY: State University of New York Press.

Hess, F. M. (2003, January). *A license to lead? A new leadership agenda for America's schools*. Washington, DC: Progressive Policy Institute.

Hess, F. M., & Kelly, A. P. (2005). The accidental principal: What doesn't get taught at ed schools? *Education Next, 5*(3), *34-40*.

Hirth, M. A. (1988). *Principals' knowledge of Public Law 94-142 and significant court litigation in the area of special education* (Doctoral dissertation). Available from ProQuest Dissertations and Theses database. (UMI No. 8904614)

Individuals with Disabilities Education Improvement Act of 2004 (Public Law No. 108-446). 20 U.S.C. § 1400 *et seq.*

Interstate School Leaders Licensure Consortium. (1996). *Standards for school leaders*. Washington, DC: Council of Chief State School Officers.

Keith, D. L. (2011). Principal desirability for professional development. *Academy of Educational Leadership Journal, 15*(2), 95-128.

Keyes, M. W., Hanley-Maxwell, C., & Capper, C. A. (1999). "Spirituality? It's the core of my leadership": Empowering leadership in an inclusive elementary school. *Educational Administration Quarterly, 35*(2), 203-237.

Krajewski, B., & Krajewski, L. (2000). Inclusion planning strategies: Equalizing opportunities for cognitively disabled students. *NASSP Bulletin, 84*(513), 48-53.

Larson, C., & Ovando, C. (2001). *The color of bureaucracy: The politics of equity in multicultural school communities*. Belmont, CA: Wadsworth.

Lashley, C. (2007). Principal leadership for special education: An ethical framework. *Exceptionality, 15*(3), 177-187.

Laskey, B., & Karge, B. D. (2006, March). Meeting the needs of students with disabilities: Experience and confidence of principals. *NASSP Bulletin, 90*(1), 19-36.

Leithwood, K., & Steinbach, R. (2003). Toward a second generation of school leadership standards. In P. Hallinger (Ed.), *Reshaping the landscape of school leadership development: A global perspective* (pp. 257-272). Lisse, The Netherlands: Swets and Zeitlinger.

Lust, C. (2005). *Principal preparation, knowledge, and understanding of special education as a social justice issue* (Doctoral dissertation). Available from ProQuest Dissertations and Theses database. (UMI No. 3233915)

Marshall, C., & Gerstl-Pepin, C. (2005). *Re-framing educational politics for social justice.* Boston, MA: Allyn & Bacon, Pearson Education.

McClard-Bertrand, L. A., & Bratberg, W. D. (2007, October 17). Promoting the success of all students: The principal's role in providing quality special education services. *Academic Leadership, 5*(3). Retrieved from http://www.academicleadership.org/emprical_research/Promoting_the_Success_of_All_Students.shtml

McKenzie, K., Christman, D., Hernandez, F., Fierro, E., Capper, C., Dantley, M., ... Scheurich, J. (2008). Educating leaders for social justice: A design for a comprehensive, social justice leadership preparation program. *Educational Administration Quarterly, 44*(1), 11-138.

Murphy, J. (2005). Unpacking the foundations of ISLLC Standards and addressing concerns in the academic community. *Educational Administration Quarterly, 41*, 154-191.

Murphy, J., Yff, J., & Shipman, N. (2000). Implementation of the Interstate School Leaders Licensure Consortium Standards. *International Journal of Leadership in Education, 3*(1), 17-39.

Nardone, A. J. (1999). *The campus administrator as instructional leader in acquisition of knowledge of special education legal issues* (Doctoral dissertation). Available from ProQuest Dissertations and Theses database. (UMI No. 9926870)

Office of Program Policy Analysis and Government Accountability. (2000, January). *OPPAGA program review: Management training act should be revised* (Report No. 99-26). Tallahassee, FL: Author.

Patterson, J., Marshall, C., & Bowling, D. (2000). Are principals prepared to manage special education dilemmas? *NASSP Bulletin, 84*(613), 9-20.

Potter, L., & Hulsey, D. E. (2001). Tips for principals to improve their special education programs. *In CASE, 2*, 2-7.

Power, D. M. (2007). *A study of selected Virginia school principals' knowledge of special education law* (Doctoral dissertation). Available from ProQuest Dissertations and Theses database. (UMI No. 3347623)

Praisner, C. L. (2003). Attitudes of elementary school principals toward the inclusion of students with disabilities. *Exceptional Children, 69*, 135-145.

Rhys, H. J. (1996). *The principal's role in special education: Building-level administrators' knowledge of special education issues as these apply to their administrative role* (Doctoral dissertation). Available from ProQuest Dissertations and Theses database. (UMI No. 9637342)

Rosener, J. B. (1990). Ways women lead. *Harvard Business Review, 68*(6), 119-25.

Shapiro, J. P., & Stefkovich, J. A. (2005). *Ethical leadership and decision making in education: Applying theoretical perspectives to complex dilemmas* (2nd ed.). Mahwah, NJ: Erlbaum.

Smith, J. O., & Colon, R. J. (1998). Legal responsibilities toward students with disabilities: What every administrator should know. *NASSP Bulletin, 82*(594), 40-53.

Strike, K., & Soltis, J. F. (1992). *The ethics of teaching* (2nd ed.). New York, NY: Teachers College Press.

Valesky, T. C., & Hirth, M. A. (1992). Survey of the states: Special education knowledge requirements for school administrators. *Exceptional Children, 58*(5), 399-406.

Wakeman, S., Browder, D., Meier, I., & McColl, A. (2007). The implications of No Child Left Behind for students with developmental disabilities. *Mental Retardation and Developmental Disabilities Research Reviews, 13*, 143-150.

Wakeman, S. L. (2005*). Principal knowledge of fundamental and current issues in special education* (Doctoral dissertation). Available from ProQuest Dissertations and Theses database. (UMI No. 3161854)

Young, I. (1990). *Justice and the politics of difference.* Princeton, NJ: Princeton University Press.

Young, M., Mountford, M., & Skrla, L. (2006). Infusing gender and diversity issues into educational leadership programs: Transformational learning and resistance. *Journal of Educational Administration, 44*(3), 264-277.

CHAPTER 5

FUTURE DIRECTIONS FOR RESEARCH IN LEARNING AND TEACHING IN EDUCATIONAL LEADERSHIP

Liz Hollingworth

ABSTRACT

The final chapter summarizes the common threads running through the three studies and gives directions to the field for future research in learning and teaching in educational leadership, such as partnerships with local school districts and mindful internship placement. Best practices in program evaluation, including candidate assessment, personnel evaluation of faculty, and curriculum evaluation are described, and suggestions for research still needed to be conducted by future doctoral scholars are outlined.

RESEARCH IN LEARNING AND TEACHING IN EDUCATIONAL LEADERSHIP

The Kottkamp Award was created to encourage and highlight the research of new scholars to the field of educational leadership engaged in program evaluation research. The three chapters in this volume, written

Research in Learning and Teaching in Educational Leadership
pp. 127–133
127

by newly minted doctoral scholars and their senior advisors give a glimpse into the current research directions that are informing the field.

The era of high-stakes accountability has pressured school leaders in unexpected ways; for example, leaders now need to know how to use a plethora of information, including student achievement test score data, to make decisions, requiring a shift for traditional preparation programs. The three award-winning studies described in this volume provide examples of methods for conducting research in best practices in leadership preparation for the 21st century. In the tradition of high quality program evaluation, both qualitative and quantitative data are used to understand the efficacy of three different educational leadership programs.

Educational Leadership Program Evaluation

There are three components to evaluating the efficacy of educational leadership preparation programs: candidate assessment, personnel evaluation of faculty, and the evaluation of the curriculum (see Figure 5.1). Although the data used for each might overlap, it is important not to confuse the purposes of each of the three kinds. First, candidate assessment is designed to determine whether individual students have met the requirements for licensure and graduation from a preparation program. Using admissions data as pretest information and end of program requirements as posttest, evaluators can pair that information with course grades and internship evaluations to determine whether or not a student is ready to lead a school. Second, personnel evaluation is conducted on everyone in the program, including adjuncts, mentors, and field supervisors. Program evaluators can use information about the selection process, student evaluation, teaching observations, and retention to make informed decisions about retention and promotion. The third component, curriculum evaluation, requires a data system to track student graduation rates and job placements. Programs must regularly and systematically gather data from graduates on the strengths and weaknesses of the preparation program. Feedback on the curriculum can come from an advisory group of practitioners, graduates, and other stakeholders.

Surveys are a common way to gather data from graduates about the utility of the training they received from their preparation programs. A task force of the Learning and Teaching in Educational Leadership Special Interest Group was created to build a set of evaluation tools for leadership preparation programs to use. This subcommittee grew into the University Council for Educational Administration National Center for the Evaluation of Educational Leadership Preparation and Practice,

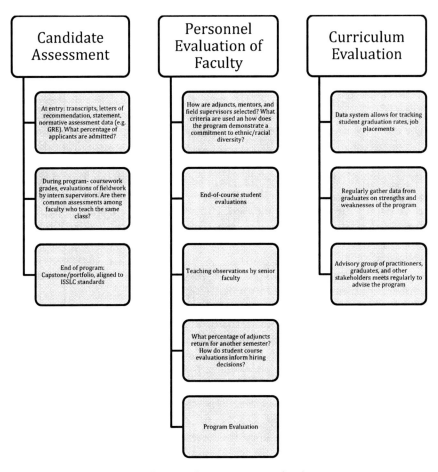

Figure 5.1.   Components of a complete program evaluation.

which administers the School Leadership Preparation and Practice Survey (SLPPS). This survey gives the designers of leadership preparation programs information on program graduates and alumni and allows for the comparison of graduates' experiences across programs. In addition to survey data, programs find it useful to conduct periodic focus group interviews with graduates.

The variables used to evaluate the preparation programs need to be within the control of the program, like admission test scores, student course evaluations, and candidate placement rates after graduation, and not K-12 student achievement test scores, which are beyond the scope of the preparation program's reach.[1]

Common Themes: The Internship Experience

The common theme that emerged from this volume's three studies is the need for mindful internship experiences where candidates experience personal transformation. In Chapter 2, the need for superintendents to have mentors in their beginning years once they have graduated was cited as a suggestion for improving preparation, despite the fact that most preparation programs lack the capacity to mentor candidates postgraduation. Along the lines of site-based, context-dependent mentoring, Chapter 3 described a program that moved beyond coteaching with practitioners to a grow-your-own, site-based program embedded within a school district. This was partially a reaction to the perceived shortcomings of traditional preparation programs that did not have job-embedded training aligned with district goals.

The lack of a built-in evaluation system for that program was determined to be a weakness, but in truth, until it was legislatively mandated, university preparation programs did not readily engage in self-evaluation either. In fact, it is precisely this area, judging preparation program quality, which has become a fertile ground for research, inspiring the University Council of Educational Administration to sponsor the *Journal of Research in Leadership Education,* a peer-reviewed journal published by SAGE.

Chapter 4 explains the need for instructional leadership training as a social justice issue, specifically with regard to the needs of students with a special education designation. In fact, only 7% of the study participants reported that their preparation programs had provided them with the job-related training they needed in the area of special education. The provision of instructional leadership experiences during the internship would address this concern. However, an unexplored question is the qualifications of mentor leaders in the field of special education. Should programs require internship hours with the special education coordinators to ensure candidates are graduating with the requisite knowledge in the field?

In short, the common themes from the studies in this volume center around the intentionality of field experiences and the need for preparation programs to partner closely with schools to ensure leaders are exposed to a breadth of activities to give them the skills they will need as novice principals and superintendents. The field of educational administration needs further research, in particular longitudinal research on the best methods for organizing the internships given the changing political pressures for student achievement accountability. In preparation for this work, most scholars who conduct research in learning and teaching in educational leadership draw upon the same foundational literature.

Common Literature Informing
Research on Leadership Preparation

Most program evaluation research papers in educational leadership have very similar literature reviews. The foundational piece for most work is McCarthy's chapter in the *Handbook of Research on Educational Administration* in 1999:

- McCarthy, M. (1999). The evolution of educational leadership preparation programs. *Handbook of research on educational administration* (Vol. 2, pp. 119-139). San Francisco, CA: Jossey-Bass.

Since then, there have been two important reviews of research on effective leadership preparation:

- Murphy, J., & Vriesenga, M. P. (2004). *Research on preparation programs in educational administration: An analysis*. Columbia, MO: University Council for Educational Administration.
- Young, M., Crow, G.M., Murphy, J., & Ogawa, R. (2009). *Handbook of research on the education of school leaders*. New York, NY: Routledge.

When authors address the criticisms of university-based educational leadership programs, two pieces are typically cited:

- Levine, A. (2005). *Educating school leaders*. New York, NY: The Education Schools Project.
- Hess, F. M., & Kelly, A. P. (2005). The accidental principal: What doesn't get taught at ed schools? *Education Next, 5*(3), 34-40.

Since McCarthy's call for more research on educational leadership program evaluation, the researchers preparing leaders in Chicago wrote a book that describes not only the development process, but also the evaluation methods:

- Bryk, A. S., Sebring, P. B., Allensworth, E., Easton, J. Q., & Lup-pescu, S. (2010). *Organizing schools for improvement: Lessons from Chicago*. University of Chicago Press.

The special issue of *Educational Administration Quarterly, 47*(1), dedicated to program evaluation, provides another fruitful place for scholars seeking methodological models for this research. The rationale for this work is typically cited from the introductory chapter by the editor of the special issue:

- Pounder, D. G. (2011). Leader preparation special issue: Implications for policy, practice, and research. *Educational Administration Quarterly, 47*(1), 258-267.

Final Thoughts

There are many research questions left for the field to explore: What incentives do preparation programs have to support their graduates once they have been hired to lead a school? How do online, distance preparation programs ensure that candidates are receiving high-quality internship experiences? What large-scale data sets about preparation programs should be created to allow for comparisons of program type? How can the School Leadership Preparation and Practice Survey support individual preparation programs in their quest for improvement?

Mentorship and supervised practical, hands-on experiences are the keys to good leadership preparation. Preparation programs are tasked with the difficult job of providing candidates with a myriad of experiences across multiple contexts to provide them with exposure to as many administrative cultures and leadership behaviors as possible. It is important that policymakers do not expect preparation programs to carry this burden alone; in-service professional development is probably the next phase for the field.

NOTE

1. For a technical explanation of the problems with policies that require student test scores to evaluate principals, see Fuller, E., & Hollingworth, L. (in press). A bridge too far? Challenges in evaluating principal effectiveness. *Educational Administration Quarterly*.

REFERENCES

Bryk, A. S., Sebring, P. B., Allensworth, E., Easton, J. Q., & Luppescu, S. (2010). *Organizing schools for improvement: Lessons from Chicago*. Chicago, IL: University of Chicago Press.

Fuller, E., & Hollingworth, L. (in press). A bridge too far? Challenges in evaluating principal effectiveness. *Educational Administration Quarterly*.

Hess, F. M., & Kelly, A. P. (2005). The accidental principal: What doesn't get taught at ed schools? *Education Next*, *5*(3), 34-40.

Levine, A. (2005). *Educating school leaders*. New York, NY: The Education Schools Project.

Murphy, J., & Vriesenga, M. P. (2004). *Research on preparation programs in educational administration: An analysis*. Columbia, MO: University Council for Educational Administration.

McCarthy, M. (1999). The evolution of educational leadership preparation programs. *Handbook of research on educational administration* (Vol. 2, pp. 119-139). San Francisco, CA: Jossey-Bass.

Pounder, D. G. (2011). Leader preparation special issue: Implications for policy, practice, and research. *Educational Administration Quarterly*, *47*(1), 258-267.

Young, M., Crow, G. M., Murphy, J., & Ogawa, R. (2009). *Handbook of research on the education of school leaders*. New York, NY: Routledge.

ABOUT THE AUTHORS

Arnold Danzig is a professor of education leadership and policy and founding director of the doctoral program in educational leadership at San Jose State University. He is a professor emeritus from Arizona State University and served in multiple positions at ASU including associate dean and division director in the Mary Lou Fulton College of Education and associate director of the School of Public Affairs. His research on leadership offers a humanistic vision of leadership for democratic institutions, with commitment to the betterment of individual and institutional lives. He has authored or co-authored books, chapters, and articles on leadership; he is also an editor of the 2012 volume of the *Review of Research in Education* on the theme of "Education, Democracy, and the Public Good" published in collaboration with the American Educational Research Association, and forthcoming 2014 volume on language policy and politics in education.

Arthur J. Fessler is superintendent of Community Consolidated School District 59 in Arlington Heights, Illinois. His research interests include principal and superintendent leadership preparation and leadership for learning. He was the 2012 recipient of the Robert Kottkamp Outstanding Dissertation Award of the Learning and Teaching in Educational Leadership Special Interest Group of the American Educational Research Association.

Donald G. Hackmann is a professor of educational administration in the Department of Education Policy, Organization, and Leadership at the University of Illinois at Urbana-Champaign. His research interests include leadership preparation programs and faculty characteristics, the principalship, and promoting college-career readiness.

Liz Hollingworth, PhD, is an associate professor in the Educational Policy and Leadership Studies Department at the University of Iowa, where she also serves as an associate director in the Center for Evaluation and Assessment. Her research focuses on issues of leadership, assessment, and program evaluation. In particular, her work explores how federal school reform policies affect classroom practice and school administration. Professor Hollingworth has served as the secretary and program cochair for the Learning and Teaching in Educational Leadership Special Interest Group prior to being elected as chair.

Lindsay Jesteadt, PhD, is an Associate Graduate Faculty member in the Department of Educational Leadership and Research Methodology at Florida Atlantic University. Prior to that she spent nine years in K12 education as a special education teacher, team leader, and mainstream consultant responsible for IDEA compliance at the school level. She has worked in all levels of K12 education, from elementary through high school, and most recently at a separate day school for students with emotional/behavioral disabilities. Dr. Jesteadt's research interests focus on principal preparation programs, special education training for school administrators, and teacher evaluations. She was the 2013 recipient of the Robert Kottkamp Outstanding Dissertation Award of the Learning and Teaching in Educational Leadership Special Interest Group of the American Educational Research Association.

Shawn Joseph was the recipient of the American Educational Research Association's Outstanding Dissertation Award in the area of educational leadership and is currently the superintendent of the Seaford School District in Delaware. Dr. Joseph has served as an adjunct professor for The George Washington University and McDaniel College. His research interests include principal preparation, principal development, school improvement planning, and school/community relationships. He was the 2011 recipient of the Robert Kottkamp Outstanding Dissertation Award of the Learning and Teaching in Educational Leadership Special Interest Group of the American Educational Research Association.

Meredith Mountford, PhD, is an associate professor at Florida Atlantic University in the Department of Educational Leadership and Research Methodology. She is also director of UCEA's Center for Research on School District Governance and Chair of AERA's Research on the Superintendency SIG. She is internationally recognized for her work on school boards and school district governance structures, processes, and systems.

Virginia Roach, EdD, is currently the dean of the Graduate School of Education at Bank Street College in New York City. Prior to joining Bank Street she was an associate professor and chair of the Department of Educational Leadership at George Washington University. Her research interests include leadership development, especially as related to culture and gender, and educational policy related to the development of school and district leaders.

CPSIA information can be obtained at www.ICGtesting.com
Printed in the USA
LVOW10s0737241013

358389LV00001B/2/P